Previous Titles

Labyrinth: Your Path to Self Discovery
(ISBN: 9780738756615)

Labyrinth Wisdom Cards
(ISBN: 9780957244702)

Death — You Gotta Love It

What People Are Saying About

Death — You Gotta Love It

If mankind better understood death and therefore life, this world would be a much easier place to live and learn. Tony Ærcyus Christie's book, *Death — You Gotta Love It*, does an excellent job of explaining the true nature of our existence and why death is not only nothing to fear but simply another milestone in our eternal evolution.
David Gaggin, author of *Our Eternal Existence*

In an extraordinary and compelling work, spiritual teacher Tony Ærcyus Christie produces a veritable manifesto for the afterlife which will change utterly your way of thinking about time, reality, and existence. He aims to shatter longstanding taboos around discussion of death and our entry into that "undiscovered country." Writing with compassion and a reassuring tone, he seeks to replace trepidation with love, and free us from the fear and mystery of the end of life. With the caring offer of ways to prepare positively for the inevitable, Tony provides a welcome route to existential solace.
Geoff Ward, writer and journalist at Medium.com, author of *Spirals: The Pattern of Existence*

In over 88 years of living in the material world, I've come to look for a paradox in everything. Author Christie explores the biggest paradox of all — that death, our greatest fear, is life's greatest gift and our most fulfilling experience. To fully appreciate that, one has to go well beyond what the churches and science have provided. That's the journey Christie takes in this very informative, interesting, and intriguing book.
Michael Tymn, author of *The Afterlife Revealed, No One Really Dies* and *Consciousness Beyond Death*

This book shines a light into the darkness where death literally lives. It lifts the lid on the conditioning and beliefs that infest our cultural conventions in relation to death and dying. The fear of death is one of the cornerstones of the control structures that have been systemically imposed on the human collective throughout our alleged history. Tony shares an intelligent awareness of the concepts involved, and many others, in ways that actually undermine those structures and the fear they rest upon. This will appeal to anyone open to questioning conventional narratives and interested in exploring further.
Altazar Rossiter PhD, author of *Developing Spiritual Intelligence* and *Partnering with Spiritual Intelligence*, explorer in consciousness, and facilitator of a "Self-Empowerment Mystery School" in the Netherlands

A deceptively simple but penetrating discussion of death which I thoroughly enjoyed. A thought-provoking, easy-to-read synthesis of many fields of research that completely reframes our understanding of dying, culminating in practical and wise advice for how to live well and die well. Highly recommended
Chris M. Bache PhD, author of *LSD and the Mind of the Universe*

In this fascinating and poignant book, bright soul Tony Ærcyus Christie guides us through his brilliant five stages of loving death and accepting that our Earth body is not ours but simply on loan to us. *Death — You Gotta Love It* shines a light on the limiting beliefs held by the collective consciousness around death and dying, introducing Death instead as a guru — helping us return to where we truly belong: love and truth. Well researched, profound, and deeply enlightening — a true pleasure to read. I highly recommend it.
Susan Browne, creator of Angel EFT and author of *Ask Your Angel Guides*

Death — You Gotta Love It

Choosing Love over Fear in Life's Greatest Transition

Tony Ærcyus Christie

BOOKS

London, UK
Washington, DC, USA

CollectiveInk

First published by O-Books, 2026
O-Books is an imprint of Collective Ink Ltd.,
Unit 11, Shepperton House, 89 Shepperton Road, London, N1 3DF
office@collectiveinkbooks.com
www.collectiveinkbooks.com
www.o-books.com

For distributor details and how to order, please visit the 'Ordering' section on our website.

ISBN: 978 1 917704 44 1
978 1 917991 08 7 (ebook)
Library of Congress Control Number: 2025940414

A CIP catalogue record for this book is available from the British Library.

Design: Lapiz Digital Services

UK: Printed and bound by CPI Group (UK) Ltd, Croydon, CR0 4YY
Printed in North America by CPI GPS partners

The manufacturer's authorised representative in the EU for product safety is:
eucomply OÜ - Pärnu mnt 139b-14, 11317 Tallinn, Estonia,
hello@ eucompliancepartner.com, www.eucompliancepartner.com

Contents

Foreword

I just want to be loved. You cannot know the pain it causes me for you to fear me. There is so much to me that you do not know, and even more that you have wrong about me.

This book about loving death fills me with joy. It shares my true self with you, without all the preconceived ideas and images that you have of me. It looks into my heart to find the beauty that resides there. Here is an opportunity for you to get to know me better and to make up your own mind about who I am and what I am about.

I do not understand why you portray me in fearful and sometimes repulsive images. You often hide me in a black hooded cloak, keeping my face hidden, with bony fingers holding a scythe as if I have to cut and harvest something.

That is not me. That is your own fear that you are portraying. The fearful skeletal-type portraits that you create of me are merely portrayals of the lack of substance in your understanding of me. There is so much more to me.

I am a lady of compassion. I come to you at times of transition. I come to you with love and support. I come to help you return home to a knowing and realization of who you really are. When you get to know me, you get to know yourself. I am here to help you remember who you are.

In getting to know me, you see behind all the fearful events and qualities that are frequently laid at my door. In coming to love me, you see beyond the demise of the physical body. In experiencing me, you know eternal life. For I am not the wasting of the flesh, or the physical pain that accompanies illness.

I am not the grief that aches your heart when a loved one dies. I am the joy beneath those tears. I am not the tears that flow with love; I am the love in those tears. I am not the emptiness that permeates your being; I am the fullness of life.

I am the facilitator of life. Many of you decry me, yet few of you even consider what it would be like to live forever in a physical body. Perhaps it would be mind-numbingly dull to have no change in how you experience life. As the purveyor of an end to this physical existence, I bring you into the knowing of eternal life. You cannot die; you just change.

Change keeps you alive. It brings vibrancy. It brings newness and wonder to the world around you. The fear of change is the fear of life. So, I am here to help you remember that you have a choice. You may choose fear, or you may choose to let go of your fears, including your fear of me.

As you let go of your fears, you begin to see me for who I really am. You begin to see that I am working with you, not against you. You begin to know more about yourself, for I am your greatest teacher. You begin to live a life from your center of love, from the vibrancy that is always within you. And when you finally choose to move on from the physical body that you now occupy, you come to ask me for my services from that place of love and joy.

For I am here to serve you. My service is a service of love. My service is freely given, whether you ask it of me, or not. You have nothing to fear. As you move through the pages of this book, you will see and learn not only how I am of service, but how you come to let go of your fears about me. For in the end, there is no fear — only Love. And I am Love. I am the ending and the beginning. Embrace me, my love.

In Love, Power, and Wisdom,
DEATH

Acknowledgments

My heartfelt thanks to the many people who helped and inspired me throughout the writing of this book. First and foremost, eternal gratitude to my wife, Fionnuala, whose ever-present love, encouragement, and support were an essential ingredient in getting this book to completion. Thank you to my children: Cara, Eoghan, Cillian, and Aoibhinn, and Fionnuala's children: Linda, Lisa, Rob, and Jack, for their love, courage, and input into the book as it progressed through its many stages.

Deepest thanks to my dear friend of many lifetimes, Carin Wennink, for reading an early version of the manuscript and making many helpful suggestions. A special thanks to DC Bonavoglia for her editing expertise. My deepest gratitude to everyone at Collective Ink for bringing this book to you.

Loving thanks to the many authors whose works and insights into life, death, and dying inspired me and prompted me to embark on bringing forward this approach to death for the benefit of all. And finally, to Death herself for her guidance, inspiration, and insights into the greater meaning of death and life.

Chapter 1

The Birth of Death

The day you are born is the day you die. If you weren't born, you wouldn't die. We traditionally celebrate birth and mourn death. Yet birth is the start of death. At birth, the one who is born cries, and everyone laughs. At death, everyone cries except the one who has died. Perhaps the newborn baby knows more than those who have spent many years on Earth.

When one thing ends, another begins. There is no ending without a beginning of something else. Birth and death are inseparable stages on a continuum; stages in a greater journey that you are experiencing. When you see death as part of a greater whole and not an end in itself, you begin to tap into a greater sense of understanding of your existence.

Birth and death are both beginnings. Birth is the beginning of your life experiencing a physical body. Death is the beginning of you experiencing life beyond the physical. Death is a birth, or a rebirth, into the nonphysical world where you realize that you always existed. Death is the doorway inviting you to walk through into the next phase of your life.

Life and death are not opposites. Life has no opposite. Life always is and always will be. Life is more than this lifetime. Death is just a moment in life, and the act of death merely changes that life to another form of expression. When you see all life as a series of beginnings, there are no endings; only openings into something new.

Death has always been with us, yet its presence appears to be diminishing. Death is now mostly hidden away and not talked about or considered until it rears its beautiful head right in front of us. Its existence is commonly ignored and even denied. Death is becoming increasingly invisible, and we are encouraged to live our lives as if we are going to live in a physical body forever. As more deaths are happening in hospitals, people are becoming more removed from the experience of death, and it is increasingly becoming a taboo subject.

The health services in many Western countries see death as a failure. The futility of this approach instills fear into the hearts of both doctors and their patients. Most health services see themselves as a service to battle, conquer, and defeat illness and death. Many of us have handed over our power and control to the doctors, who in the face of ultimate death are as helpless and powerless as ourselves. When death comes, we have also handed over our power to undertakers, funeral directors, and the lawmakers around death and dead bodies. Increasingly, we have abandoned the dead, and in so doing, we have abandoned ourselves.

With so many developments in technology, we as a society are coming to expect a fix or cure for everything. As a result, we can resent illness and death when a cure is not readily available. We may seek someone or something to blame, especially if we feel vulnerable, fearful, traumatized, or angry. We expect that in a modern world we should not have to feel this way. We want a reason, explanation, or answer as to why this "tragedy" should have happened. In our search for answers, we often look in the wrong place.

Rather than looking more closely at death, we are prompted to divert our attention elsewhere. The marketing and salespeople of the world have a vested interest in keeping us from changing our thinking around death. Many products are sold to keep us looking and feeling younger, playing on our fear of growing old and dying. There is little profit to be made in being happy with an aging body. There is even less if we do not fear death. Yet the solution of delaying and deferring the realization of our approaching death does not bring contentment.

The avoidance of death is a cultural failing. Pretending it does not exist only serves to increase the fears surrounding death. It is time for a rethink. It's OK for your body to slow down. It's OK for your hair to thin and recede. It's OK for you to have wrinkles on your face. Not only is it OK, but it is also to be enjoyed. Learning to enjoy the creaking body, the aging wrinkles, and the diminishing vitality puts the power back into your own hands.

As you allow yourself to be fully present with the gradual demise of the physical body, you are opening yourself to all that death brings. In the face of society's current views on death, this path is not for the faint-hearted. Facing death takes courage. It brings up a range of thoughts and feelings that many choose to avoid or deny. Yet this sometimes-difficult search for understanding is also a search for buried treasure. You are a pioneer in search of discoveries. As you explore death, you are at the forefront of those seeking a different approach to death — the Golden Death.

Death is born when you lose your connection to Source, to your divine infinite self. This sometimes happens at physical birth, but also occurs during your lifetime when you are disconnected from your true state of being. The birth of death is the birth of an opportunity for you to choose differently how you relate to death. It is an opportunity to give death a rebirth and for you to reclaim your death from the negative thoughts and emotions surrounding it. In choosing to see death differently, you are creating a new vision and ultimately a new experience of death for yourself. Just as you can be reborn into a new way of life, you can also "re-die" into a new way of dying. Learning as much as you can about death is the start of your re-death, and your rebirth.

Approaching Death

Death is something we all face. While you do not have a choice in experiencing death, you have a choice as to how you see and think about death. Your current approach to death and your ongoing existence after death falls into one of three categories, two of which are encapsulated in the words of Thomas Aquinas, who said, "To one who has faith, no explanation is necessary. To one without faith, no explanation is possible." So, you are either a believer in a hereafter, a non-believer, or somewhere in between.

Whichever of the aforementioned categories you fall into, if you are open-minded and willing to consider all the information in this book, then you are embarking on a journey of exploration and adventure. If you can change even slightly your thinking about death, you are opening up a new approach to life.

The more informed you are about death and its many aspects, the more you take control of your attitudes and approach to death. The more you learn about the different thoughts and beliefs of what happens before, during, and after death, the better you can formulate your thinking, attitudes, and behavior towards death. The more you learn about death, the more you learn about life. The more you learn about where you might be going, the more you learn about where you might have come from, and what life is all about.

Life, including death, is a journey of exploration. Do not expect that you will automatically know what to do at the time of your death. Being informed and prepared makes the journey not just easier, but genuinely more enjoyable. If you were going on an adventure holiday to a new and strange place that you knew little about, you would spend time informing yourself and checking out the best way to get there and the best things to do when there.

Likewise, the more you plan for your death trip, the more enjoyable and easier the journey becomes. When you know the route that you are going to take, it brings a sense of peace and comfort to know how to get there. When you arrive at your destination, you have everything arranged and organized so that you have a clear picture in your head of what is to happen.

It is as if you are going back to a place where you have been on holiday many times before, and you know the people, the places, and the process for everything to go smoothly. You have no fear, as you know that you have prepared as best you can. You look forward with positive expectations and excitement to making your death journey.

Elisabeth Kübler-Ross, in her groundbreaking book *On Death and Dying,* described five stages or approaches to death and dying. Most people who are faced with a terminal illness go through some or all of these. These are denial, anger, bargaining, depression, and acceptance (Kübler-Ross 1969). Even those who are in good health and not faced with a terminal illness will often have their approach to death in one of those five stages. These stages are not linear, and you may feel one or more of these at various times as you are faced with death.

The first stage of denial can be seen as a coping mechanism that allows only what you can handle to arise. Whether concerning your impending death or the death of a loved one, the feeling of "it can't be happening to me" or "it can't be true" is typical of the denial of death.

Anger is an indication of the intensity of thoughts and feelings you may be experiencing towards death. Anger is sometimes expressed in the question "Why me?" Feelings of helplessness and lashing out at some unseen force that is bringing a huge shift in your life experience often manifest as anger.

Bargaining is an attempt to see and have things differently. It can manifest in attempts to postpone death through changes in behavior and attitudes. Bargaining helps to bring an awareness of the reality of death, yet it also carries a sense that it can be postponed through some commitments or actions.

Depression involves the realization in the present of the perceived emptiness of death. During this phase, you may experience profound sadness, hopelessness, and emotional pain as you begin to fully grasp the reality and permanence of your perceived loss. This stage is marked by feelings of isolation, withdrawal from activities, and a deep sense of mourning.

Acceptance entails acknowledging the reality that this physical life ends and is a way of living with that realization. It allows you to live again without denial, anger, bargaining, or depression.

These five states are predominantly external to your true self. They look at death as if death is something outside of you, not something deep within you. An outside view of death gives the impression that it is something that will not happen to you. From an external observer viewpoint, the consequences are to see death as final, often encompassing pain and suffering, and engulfed in upset and fear.

When you internalize death, you acknowledge death as an integral part of you. You are no longer a passive bystander but have become an active participant in your death. By making death an "inside job," you unlock new ways of understanding and being with death — the stages of loving death.

The Five Stages of Loving Death

The five stages of loving death are: Allowance, Peace, Gratitude, Love, and Celebration. They invite you to move beyond merely coping towards a transformative relationship with death and an empowering relationship with life. These stages emphasize not just surviving death and grief, but integrating them into life with openness, awareness, and meaning.

Allowance is the stage where a person consciously gives themselves permission to fully feel and experience the reality of death, instead of resisting, denying, or merely accepting it. In this stage, there is an openness to acknowledging all emotions around death without judgment. It goes beyond acceptance in that one is the impartial observer of death and its associated emotions. Allowance does not assign any qualities to death. In allowance, we open ourselves to the understanding that death is not merely an end, but a natural part of existence that touches all living beings. This stage doesn't demand immediate comfort or ease with death but rather invites us to allow mortality to exist alongside our daily experiences, creating a foundation for deeper engagement with life.

Peace is a profound inner calm that arises when we go beyond our intellectual understanding of death and enter a state of genuine stillness. This stage manifests as a deep reconciliation with mortality that transcends mere allowance. In peace, the anxious chatter of the mind quietens, and we experience moments of genuine tranquility when contemplating our finite earthly nature. This isn't a passive resignation but an active harmony; a recognition that we are part of something larger than ourselves, connected to cycles of existence that extend beyond our individual lives. It allows us to hold the paradox of fully embracing earthly life while acknowledging its impermanence, creating space for a serene coexistence with the knowledge of our mortality.

Gratitude emerges as we deepen our relationship with mortality, shifting our perspective to one of appreciation. In this stage, we begin to recognize the profound gifts that death offers: the heightened appreciation for each moment, the clarity about what truly matters, and the deepened connections with loved ones. Gratitude involves acknowledging how the nature of life makes each experience precious and unrepeatable. We feel thankful for the transition that is death and reflect on the positive impact that death has on our lives.

Love represents a transformative stage in our relationship with death, where we move to a genuine affection for mortality's role in our earthly lives. In this stage, we come to cherish death as a sacred teacher and companion that gives meaning to our existence. Love for death manifests as a profound appreciation for how mortality's presence enhances our capacity for connection and authenticity. When we love death, we also love life. This stage allows us to approach mortality with the same openheartedness we bring to other beloved aspects of our human experience.

Celebration represents the pinnacle of loving death, where we embrace death with openness, genuine reverence, and joy. In this stage, we actively commemorate the role death plays in creating meaning and beauty in our lives. By celebrating death, we integrate mortality into our lived experience, allowing it to infuse our days with authenticity and a profound appreciation for the miracle of consciousness. The joy of death arises from an appreciation of its role in the ongoing cycle of life, bringing a sense of liberation, transformation, and renewal. In celebrating death, we acknowledge its power to bring peace and open the way for new beginnings, both for the departed and for those who remain. Ultimately, this perspective fosters a profound appreciation for the mystery and continuity that death brings to the human journey.

These five stages of loving death are the foundation of this book. They flow between the lines — silent yet present. The progression through them in life is primarily linear, although you may experience one or more of them at any time in your conscious awareness of death. Yet, before we can truly embrace the states of loving and celebrating death, we will first explore what might be holding us back. In the following chapters, we will examine two of these obstacles: change and fear.

Chapter 2

Change

Everything is always changing. Some things change faster than others, and some change is imperceptible. Change is encapsulated in the Buddhist concept of impermanence, and is the understanding that all phenomena, including experiences, emotions, and material existence, are in a constant state of flux and change.

When you integrate impermanence into your thinking and way of being, your sense of loss as things change and at death is greatly diminished. Impermanence is sometimes called the "Law of Change and Becoming." Just as there is constant change and dissolving, there is also constant "becoming." The presence of both provides balance and harmony.

The gift of impermanence, according to Buddhist teacher Frank Ostaseski, is that

> it places us squarely in the here and now. We know that birth will end in death. Reflecting on this might cause us to savor the moment, to imbue our lives with more appreciation and gratitude. We know that the end of all accumulation is dispersion. Reflecting on this might keep us from being overwhelmed by grief and inspire us to distinguish love from attachment.
> (Ostaseski 2017)

Humanity is on a journey of expansion and growth. We are continually evolving. When you compare now to hundreds of years ago, despite the ongoing conflicts in the world, there is much greater cooperation among people and nations. The internet has enabled a huge shift in how people connect and work together. Humanity is moving inexorably towards greater unity and cooperation. This is not always a straight upward trajectory, as conflicts, differences, and divisions are backward steps in this growth. Yet, as some people and countries take one step backward, humanity as a whole is taking two steps forward.

Humanity can only advance when individuals advance. The advances and changes that individuals make reverberate throughout humanity. While it can take a great individual to bring about great change, each one of us can bring about small changes in the things that we say and do. Many small changes together make a big change. Change is all down to what each one of us does personally and individually.

Great individuals have brought about great changes in the world. The Buddha, Socrates, Jesus, Mary Magdalene, Muhammad, Mahatma Gandhi, Anandamayi Ma, Hildegard of Bingen, Teresa of Avila, Martin Luther King, and many others changed the way we think and how societies function. They may not always have been accepted at first, but their legacy resonates through the history of humankind.

When you are aware of the ever-changing world around you, you are more open to the thinking that death is just another change. How you view your existence is a key factor in how you view death. If you see yourself as just a physical body, then at death, that is the end of you. If you see yourself as consciousness that is currently inhabiting a physical body, then the question arises of what happens to this consciousness when your physical body dies. If you recognize that there is a reality beyond the physical, this informs your view of death.

Changing your approach to death and the death process is about bringing death more into the open, making it easier to speak about death, and helping remove some of the discomfort that often accompanies talking about death. It is about realizing that death makes sense: that it is a natural progression. Knowing about death helps you to dispel the fear around death, helping to lighten the sorrows that weigh down the human heart, while learning to understand life and making you feel more alive.

It can take a conscious effort to pause and consider in what state you are currently operating. As soon as you recognize the state you are currently operating in, you also begin to realize that you are always in transition from one state of consciousness to another. You are giving yourself a choice to be fully present with the movement of consciousness, knowing that nothing is fixed or static in creation. Taking the time to pause and ponder on your state of consciousness creates an opportunity to change.

Society's attitudes and behavior towards death infiltrate our thoughts and actions. The sadness and grief that is now accepted as a normal approach to death is not the only way. There is a better way. It is time to change the "normal." It is time to change the habits and ways of treating death as a fearful, tragic, mournful end of the physical life event. Changing the approach to death begins with reexamining what life is about.

The Game of (Life and) Death

Life is a course in experiences and growth. You chose to come to Earth at this time to see how you would do in life's happenings. The events and dramas of your life are playing out in front of you, so you can learn to observe them and choose how you will respond. Adverse situations offer the prospect of discovering something about yourself. They are not necessarily negative, unless you see them so.

Young and old, rich and poor, male and female — we are all playing the game of life. Yet most are playing unconsciously. Before your birth, you chose your parents, family, the place to be born and live, jobs to do, and every other aspect of your life. Then, you promptly forgot that you chose this life. When you contemplate your life, you start to remember that the game of life has a purpose, and that you chose the experiences you would have in this game of life. You are the player in this game of being human, but it is not your physical body that plays; it is the consciousness experiencing the game through it.

The body you inhabit is a mechanism for experiencing the earthly realm. It is like a car or motorhome that you step into to have certain experiences. Your consciousness animates the body, and as soon as your consciousness leaves the body, it no longer functions. The body that you now inhabit will one day return to dust or ashes. But the consciousness that is you lives on. Thinking of life in the context of death brings clarity to the temporary nature of your time in the physical body.

You are not your body. Your body does not belong to you. You have just borrowed it from the Earth for a brief time. It is like living in a rented house. You cannot own your body because it is not yours. Your body is temporary for a reason. Attempting to preserve the temporary nature of your body serves to block the flow of life that is moving through you. Your life force is a flow of energy that existed before you entered this body and will continue after you leave this body.

The more you understand the temporary nature of the body, the less attached to it you become, and the easier it is to leave it. Having a body is not the issue. The issue is how attached you are to the body you now occupy. Attachment to anything creates a desire to hold on to it and a sense of loss when it is no more.

Your body also has its own consciousness. Your body consciousness is intelligent and wise. It knows what to do in every situation. Yet we mostly do not connect with the body's consciousness and follow its guidance. Even though you created your body's consciousness energetically in the Spirit World to work with you here in this dimension, you then forgot this as you passed through the veil of forgetfulness. The expression "Listen to your body" contains a profound wisdom that is easily dismissed as a bland platitude. When you merge your consciousness fully with your body's consciousness, you function at a higher level physically and spiritually.

So, merge with your body. It holds more truth than you can imagine. How you eat, sleep, exercise, work, and play is all a communion of you and your body. You think that you need your body to function, and you do. But more importantly, your body needs you. The mutual relationship between you and your body enables you to function in this game of life and death. By attuning to your body's rhythms in the now, you learn the art of body awareness and of letting go. When it is time to part, the separation feels natural and easy.

Chapter 3

Fear

You fear what you don't understand. Fear can be found anywhere if you look for it. Some of our greatest fears are the fear of having no money, the fear of getting sick, the fear of growing old, and the fear of failure. Yet each of these fears has an identifiable source and a possible solution. The fear of death is more insidious and intangible, which can make it difficult to know and understand.

The fear of death is also known as "death anxiety" or "thanatophobia" and can take many forms. Your fear of death may be a fear of the dying process itself, or a fear of what happens after death. The fear of judgment or not having lived what you might consider to be a good life can also contribute to a fear of death. The thoughts of not having lived life to the full, or not having fulfilled your perceived purpose, can influence how you feel about death.

The prospect of becoming nothing after death and the fear of annihilation can be frightening for some. For others, it may be the fear of the unknown, although this is more accurately considered a fear of leaving the known behind. Your comfort zone is what you now know, and the thought of leaving that comfort zone at death can be unsettling.

The fear of a painful death can be so off-putting that thinking about it is avoided. It is not just the moment of death that frightens, but the pain and suffering that might precede it. For those with responsibility for others, the fear of how your loved ones will manage without you, or not wanting them to have the pain of grieving for you, can be paramount.

Many of the fears around death can be encapsulated in the fear of loss. You may fear the loss of life, the loss of contact with loved ones, the loss of attachment to physical things, or the loss of your achievements and perceived sense of worth here on Earth, such as fame and prosperity. At death, you may have to let go of what you now consider to be a part of you, and that can be fearful. For when you let go of everything that you think makes you who you are, you may not know who you are.

Knowledge and understanding can significantly reduce these fears of death. As you read this book, you will learn about the various aspects of death, dying, and the hereafter. Death can be demystified through the knowledge that you gain, and you can transform fears around death into a source of motivation to live fully and authentically. Through understanding mortality, learning about the dying process, considering the accounts of the hereafter, and examining how you view all aspects of death and dying, you will have alleviated many of your fears around death and moved to a place where you can contemplate loving death.

Much of the fear of death comes from the images, emotions, and understanding that you have of death. Fear, dread, anxiety, worry, and more stem from ignorance; from not knowing. The collective fear of death has resulted in images of death that are frightening, sometimes sinister, and often scary. Skulls and skeletons have become symbols of the fear of death. A faceless being in a black hooded cloak, often carrying a scythe, gives the impression that death is taking something from you. Yet these images of death can only take what you give them. If you give them your power, then you will experience powerlessness and fear.

You can change the impact of these images of death by creating your own image of death. Try drawing an image of death with a smiley face and see how it feels. Dress your image of death in beautiful colors, and you begin to change the energy around death. See your image of death waving a magic wand, creating beautiful sparkling colors. See death as your fairy godmother making your wishes come true, and death begins to take on a new meaning.

The word "death" itself also gives rise to fear because of the associations many have with it. Most dictionaries describe death in terms of endings such as the "total cessation of life," "act or fact of dying," "state of being dead," "permanent ending of vital processes," and "the personification of the power that destroys life." The word "death" does not have any inherent characteristics. The word "death" holds only the meaning you attach to it. There are no emotions in death except those you ascribe to it. Death, and the word "death," are beautiful if you see them as such.

One of the first steps in overcoming your fear of death is to be willing to explore all aspects of it. If exploring your feelings around the word "death" is too worrying or distressing to even consider, then choosing another word for death can help ease those emotions. You need to be certain, however, that you are not using a different word as a means of avoiding your exploration of death.

Other terms that you may hear used, such as "the last breath," or "his final moments," are also imbued with a finality that resonates with the fear of death and its perceived ending. One way to move away from the collective fear surrounding death is to use words that more readily explain what happens at death. Words such as "transition" and "passing" and expressions such as "crossing over," "leaving the body," and "leaving the physical body" all convey a different view of the end of physical life. Using these words and terms can have the effect of seeing death differently without the associations and emotions that are attached to the word "death."

The fear that you have of death stems from your belief systems. If your beliefs are out of alignment with the infinite nature of who you are and with your path of evolution, then you will experience fear. When fear arises, consider that it may be coming up for you to look at it, to examine it, to see where it is originating, and to consider if you are out of sync with the infinite you.

If you dread the idea of looking at your fears, then they will become more prominent until you realize that some aspect of your belief system is misaligned and you need to change it. When you change or let go of the belief that is no longer true for you and now have a belief that is in harmony with who you now are, the fear will diminish and disappear. Getting more into alignment is about learning from fear and making fear your friend. Fear is one of your greatest helpers. Fear – you gotta love it.

Collective Fear

Human consciousness is currently based mainly on fear. Mainstream media news generally focuses on events and issues that induce fear. Much of the media-induced fear revolves around death. There is constant news of murders, shootings, tragedies, wars, economic collapse, energy crises, disease, and much more. The collective fear around some events is almost palpable, and it can seep into and influence your thoughts and feelings. For example, the COVID pandemic and associated media attention led to a huge collective fear in humanity.

This collective consciousness of fear affected many to the point where it became difficult to differentiate between their own personal fears and the fearful energy of the collective. This is also true about the collective fear around death. When you speak of death, or say that someone has died, you most likely are tapping into an active part of the predominant fearful energies that currently surround death.

You can separate yourself from collective fear. If you have individual fears, know also that you can free yourself from them. Freeing yourself from fear involves understanding its root causes, informing yourself as much as you can about the issue, and challenging your negative thinking about it. You build resilience through changing your thinking and how you speak until your thoughts and words result in you acting differently.

You start to free yourself from the collective fear when you realize that the fear you are feeling is not yours, and that you are picking up on the collective. The simple process of finding a quiet space and asking yourself, "Is this fear mine?" prompts an immediate response in your body and thoughts. It may take practice to be tuned into these responses and to allow the answer to become apparent to you. If you don't find it easy to do this yourself, then find someone such as a therapist who is familiar with this type of work to assist you. When you recognize that a fear is not yours, but something that you are picking up on, there are ways to disconnect from that fear.

Using the power of your intention is one of the best ways to disconnect from the collective thought-forms of fear. Take a few moments to settle and quieten yourself. Then, with your intentions, say aloud or quietly, "I disconnect from all collective fears." The energetic connections to the collective fears are like invisible cords flowing into and out of your stomach area. So, you may feel a shift of energy in your stomach area as you consciously cut these invisible cords. Use your arm like an imaginary sword and make a cutting action with your arm across the front of your body to sever any ties that you have to the collective energies. If you are in a place where doing this physically is not practical, then you can also do this action with your intention for a similar effect.

For thousands of years, humankind has been looking at the fear of death, and many spiritual teachers have been pointing another way. The Ancient Greek Stoic philosopher Epictetus taught that death is a natural part of life and that fearing it is irrational. In more recent times, Ram Dass reassured us that "dying is absolutely safe" and likened it to taking off a tight shoe (Dass 2000). Eckhart Tolle framed death as a process of stripping away all that is not truly you (Tolle 1997). These teachings point to moving away from the collective, firstly to consider your true self and identity, and then to realize your eternal nature and overcome fears.

From Fear to Love

Fear and love are opposite ends of the spectrum of energy. Fear is low-vibrational energy that separates and constricts. Love is a high vibration that is expanding and unifying. Fear is insidious. It can creep up on you and subtly dominate your thoughts and actions — so much so that you often may not realize that you are living in fear.

Fear is mind-based. It is said about the mind that it is a wonderful servant but a terrible master. The mind can take over and control you if it is allowed. On its own, the mind agonizes over death and many other life happenings. The mind will create fear and anguish around death until you cultivate a greater understanding that you have more control over your mind than you realize.

The fear of death prevents you from exploring what the hereafter may hold for you and how you can best experience what awaits you after death. Unless you study it, much of the hereafter will be new to you. Ignorance of what awaits you after death may bring up some fears. If you have learned to master your fears here on Earth, then you will be more prepared to manage any fears that surface in the hereafter.

There is another way of seeing and understanding death that allows you to live a more fulfilled life: a life of joy and love; a life of vibrancy and spontaneity; a life of purpose, wonder, and beauty. When condensed down to basics, there are only two ways of being: in fear or in love. There are only two ways of thinking, two ways of talking, two ways of acting: in love or in fear. You cannot feel fear when you are feeling love because the higher vibrational frequency of love overcomes the lower frequency of fear.

You can choose fear of death, or you can choose the antidote to fear, which is love of death. In the Bible, in the first letter of John, chapter 4, verse 18, it is said that "There is no fear in love; but perfect love casts out fear." Choosing to love rather than fear death frees and liberates you to live a fulfilled life. The Roman poet Virgil wrote that "Love conquers all, let us surrender to love" (Virgil 1999, Eclogue X: 69).

To change from having a fear of death to loving death is an empowering and enlightening transition that is life-enhancing and death-enhancing. When you love death, love of life automatically follows. Love is your "Get Out of Death Free" card.

Love is an emotion, a decision, and a way of being. To shift into a place of love in relation to death involves a process of learning. Just as you might spend time with someone you would like to get to know better, learning all about them, so it is with getting to know death. Aspects of death, such as what happens after death, what the accounts of death tell us, what we can learn from people who have been close to death, and more, all contribute to our getting to know death better. We will start this journey of exploration, not with where we go after death, but where we come from before birth.

Chapter 4

Where Do We Come From?

When you explore your possible existence before you were born, you are also exploring the issue of where you go after the death of the body. One of the most contemplated questions about death is "Where do we go when we die?" Yet there is as much, if not more, to be learned from the question "Where were we before we were born?" Studying the herebefore brings clarity to the hereafter; they are chapters of the same story.

This concept is beautifully expressed in the Gospel of Thomas, discovered in Nag Hammadi, Egypt, in 1945. When the disciples asked Yeshua (Jesus) "Tell us how our end will be?" Yeshua said: "Have you discovered the beginning and now are seeking the end? Where the beginning is, the end will be. Blessings on you who stand at the beginning. You will know the end and not taste death" (Meyer 2004).

Exploring the beginning is determined by how you see the relationship between physical matter and consciousness. If you are of the view that consciousness is a function of brain activity, then there cannot have been consciousness before the physical body existed. Then, when the physical body dies and brain function ceases, consciousness ceases to exist. If you consider consciousness to be primordial and that it can exist within and outside matter, then you can continue to exist after the death of the physical body. And if you exist after the death of the body, the consciousness that you are existed before the body was formed.

This view is supported by the first law of thermodynamics. This law states that in an enclosed system, energy can neither be created nor destroyed but can change from one form to another. When we consider that all of existence, both physical and nonphysical, is within an enclosed system, the various accounts of apparent shifts in consciousness shed light on who and where we were before we were born.

Some of the most intriguing accounts of the existence of life before we are born come from children who remember lives other than their current one. In the book *Memories of Heaven* by Wayne Dyer and Dee Garnes, there are numerous accounts of children sharing their talking with God, meeting deceased family members, choosing their parents, verifying past-life experiences, and more. The cumulative effect of these many accounts of children points strongly to evidence of a life before coming to Earth. As Dyer writes, "Young children speak their truth and recall their remembrances without any concern for what anyone else might think about it" (Dyer & Garnes 2015). There appears to be some aspect of ourselves that has existed before we were born, and that then continues after the body has died. According to Dyer, "From all that we can gather from what our children tell us, our souls are indestructible, and they transcend time and space in a way that remains mysterious to all of us."

One story recounted by Dyer comes from Elsie Farfan of Henderson, Nevada, USA. She wrote:

> When my daughter was about three years old, she mentioned in a conversation that she liked it when she was in heaven! I was a little sad that day because she had told me that she wished her daddy was home with us, like other children (we got divorced when she was a newborn). Then she said, "But that's okay, because I knew it would be like this." I asked her what she meant by that, and she answered, "Mommy, when I was in heaven, I picked you. And I knew we were going to be alone, so that's okay. Don't worry, Mommy, I love you so much." That was so amazing for me to hear.

Another story from Dyer's book is from Melissa Held-Wegner of Longmont, Colorado, USA, who wrote:

> One night at dinner, our younger foster/adopted son (he was around four years old) started talking at great length about his life "in the stars" and how he had all these brothers and sisters who lived there. He said he'd seen my husband and me from there and tried to get our attention many times, but we never could see him, so he decided to be born through his mom so we could find him. My husband and I were floored to say the least. I'd had a few miscarriages after my first son, so once my younger son told us what he'd seen, I knew his soul had been trying to come in through me even though my body was not able to do it.

Children have also recounted the events of their death experiences (also called near-death experiences or NDEs), which can shed some light on where we come from. Children's accounts of death experiences often include vivid descriptions of events that occurred while they were clinically dead or near death, such as out-of-body experiences, seeing deceased loved ones, and perceiving events from a perspective outside their physical bodies. Such experiences contribute to the consideration of the origins and continuity of consciousness.

Just as with adults, children's death experiences are very often influenced by the beliefs of the person experiencing them. They can also be influenced, and even created in the nonphysical realm, by the subconscious and collective thoughts of the society which a person has been born into or is living in. Spiritual beings encountered in the nonphysical realm can present themselves in a way that is most acceptable to the person having a death experience, and also to those to whom the experience is being retold. We are all immersed in acquired habits of perceiving, which can explain why even children experience the deities of their culture.

The bestselling book *Heaven Is for Real* details the account of Colton Burpo, as retold by his father (Burpo & Vincent 2010). Colton was not yet 4 years old in 2010 when he had an emergency appendectomy. In the months that followed, Colton told his parents that he had left his body during the surgery and was able to tell his parents exactly what they were doing in another part of the hospital at the time. He spoke about visiting Heaven and the people he met there. His parents were astonished by his descriptions and details of Heaven that matched the Bible exactly. Even though Colton was unable to read at the time of his experience, he was undoubtedly surrounded by Christian beliefs as his father, Todd, was a pastor. Notwithstanding the Christian aspects of his experience, the more common feature of his experience is the huge love that he felt.

At the University of Virginia, psychiatrist Dr Ian Stevenson, Carlson Professor of Psychiatry, and director and founder of the Division of Perpetual Studies (DOPS) in 1967, conducted extensive research into children who remember past lives. His work is being continued by Dr Jim Tucker and Dr Bruce Greyson. They now have over 2500 cases in their files.

Their research has shown that some young children, usually between the ages of 2 and 5 years, speak about memories of a previous life they claim to have lived. Cases of such young people have been found all over the world. They often also show behaviors, such as phobias or preferences, which are unusual within the context of their present-day family and cannot be explained by any current life events. These memories appear to agree with the child's statements about a previous life. In many cases of this type, the child's statements have been shown to correspond accurately to facts in the life and death of a deceased person.

About two-thirds of their cases died from unusual causes. In his book *Where Reincarnation and Biology Intersect*, Stevenson presents compelling case histories showing corresponding relationships between marks and deformities on a person's body and wounds of the person they remembered in a past life, often as a result of a violent or traumatic death. For example, a Turkish boy with a severely malformed ear said that he remembered the life of a man who was fatally wounded on the right side of the head by a shotgun discharged at close range (Stevenson 1997).

Another case was an Indian youth with several birthmarks on his chest who said he remembered the life of a man, Maha Ram, who was killed with a shotgun fired at close range. When investigated, the locations of the birthmarks were close to the wounds on the body of the man he claimed to have been.

Stevenson's research challenges the Christian belief that we live just once. It also challenges the mainstream scientific belief that reduces the mind to the brain and then asserts that the survival of consciousness after the death of the brain is impossible. It also suggests that memories can carry over after the death of the body.

There are many cases of reincarnation from India. This may be due to the widespread belief in reincarnation in India. Several of these reincarnation accounts are considered to be accurate and have even been acknowledged and recognized by members of the person's previous family.

Shanti Devi, born in Delhi, India, on 11 December 1926, claimed as a little girl to remember specific details of a past life in the village of Mathura, 150 km (90 miles) away. Although discouraged by her parents, at age 6 she ran away from home trying to reach Mathura. She said in school that she was married and had died ten days after giving birth to a child. She used words from the Mathura dialect and gave the name of her former merchant husband, Kedar Nath. The headmaster located a merchant named Kedar Nath in Mathura who had lost his wife, Lugdi Devi, nine years earlier, ten days after having given birth to a son. Kedar Nath traveled to Delhi, pretending to be his brother, but Shanti Devi immediately recognized him as Lugdi Devi's husband. She knew several details of Kedar Nath's life with his wife that convinced him that Shanti Devi was indeed the reincarnation of Lugdi Devi.

She came to public attention, and Mahatma Gandhi appointed a committee of 15 prominent citizens to investigate the case. They accompanied Shanti Devi to the village of her past-life recollections and recorded what they witnessed. The Commission supported her claim. Their report was published in 1936, saying Shanti Devi was a reincarnated child who had a past life.

In another case, Manju, a daughter of Postmaster P.N. Bharghav, who was born in Agra, said she had two houses. She did not accept her parents' house as her own. When she was 2 years old, she began talking about her real house — another house. Every time she saw a particular house in Dhuliyaganj, she claimed it was her real house. When her family took her to that house, she recounted many stories about the owner of the house and the Prakashsingh family. It was found that Manju was Prakashsingh's aunt in her previous life.

In a separate case, the *Times of India* reported the case of Manisha Devi on 4 October 2005. Manisha was born to Rampal and Khilli Devi, near Alwar in Rajasthan. The article described how Manisha had always told stories about her past life ever since she was old enough to talk. She told how she had died of typhoid and knew the color of her school belt and tie from her past birth. Her parents were puzzled as to how she could know about that when she never went to school.

She disliked being called Manisha and told her parents to call her Suman. Her story spread in the nearby villages, and some of her relatives from her past life heard about her. It came to the attention of Chaudhary Kamal Singh, Suman's father in her previous life, who lived in another village about 30 km (18 miles) away. He recalled what happened when he came to visit Manisha: "She ran into our arms when she saw us. She pointed to me and said 'voh nahi yeh mere papa hai' (Translation: He is my real father)" (*Times of India* 2005).

These accounts of a life before this lifetime not only point to a previous existence but also indicate that some form of life energy continues from one lifetime to another. There are many similar accounts of past lives that have been verified and children who remember their existence before their current life. Familiarizing yourself with the existence of a "herebefore" opens you up to seeing the hereafter in a new and different light and seeing death as a part of a continuum rather than an end in itself.

Chapter 5

Belief in Reincarnation Is Not Necessary

Several of the aforementioned cases were accounts from India, where reincarnation is a commonly held belief. In many of the accounts of reincarnation from the Western world, parents had no belief in reincarnation. Yet some Western children have given specific names, places, and events that they could never have known about, nor could they have been influenced by the concept of reincarnation.

The case of Gus Taylor, who remembers his past life as his grandfather, is fascinating. At the young age of 1½, while his dad changed his diaper, he said: "You know, when I was your age, I used to change your diaper." Gus is named after his grandfather, Augie, short for August. Whenever his family would talk about his grandpa, Gus had a very clear insistence that they were talking about him. Gus's grandfather had died a year before he was born. When Gus started talking, he kept claiming that he was his grandfather.

When he was 4 years old, he identified his grandpa's picture from a family photograph. He identified himself (as Augie) from the photo before any of his family members told him anything about it. He recognized his grandfather as a child in a large group photo. He also identified a picture of a car as the first car his grandfather ever owned.

Gus had access to information that would otherwise be impossible for him to know unless he was told. Gus claims that his sister (Augie's sister) died and became what he called a fish. What actually happened is that she was murdered, and her body was dumped into San Francisco Bay. Gus also said that after his death, God had given him a ticket that took him to a hole. It was through that hole that he traveled to his new life as

Gus Taylor. Gus also excitedly told his mom, "You know, when we die, we get to come back! I used to be big, and now I'm a kid again" (YouTube 2014).

The story of James Leininger is equally thought-provoking. Around the age of 2, James began having nightmares in which he would scream out things like "Plane on fire! Little man can't get out!" His parents, Bruce and Andrea Leininger, took note of this, and also that James gave details of planes and war tragedies that no 2-year-old boy could know.

The Leiningers put together what their son was saying and discovered that he was dreaming about and recounting episodes from the past life of World War II fighter pilot James Huston. He even gave the names of fellow pilots in his squadron. James had three G.I. Joe dolls that he named Billy, Walter, and Leon. When asked by his mother why he called them those names, he said, "Because that is who met me when I got to Heaven." Three of Huston's squadron mates who had been killed before his death were Billy Peeter, Walter Develin, and Leon Corner. Nearly everything that James said checked out. James's story is related in the book *Soul Survivor: The Reincarnation of a World War II Fighter Pilot*.

James also had memories of his time between births. Once, when Bruce hugged him, he said, "When I found you and Mommy, I knew you would be good to me." When asked, James said that he had found them in Hawaii. But when Bruce said that they all went to Hawaii that summer, James said, "It was not when we all went to Hawaii. It was just you and Mommy." James went on to say that he found them at the big pink hotel, saying, "I found you at the beach. You were eating dinner." Bruce confirmed that in 1997, he and Andrea had gone to Hawaii to celebrate their fifth wedding anniversary at the Royal Hawaiian, a big pink hotel on Waikiki Beach, and that they had a moonlight dinner on the beach on their final night. Five weeks later, she found out that she was pregnant with James (Leininger & Leininger 2010).

The Netflix documentary *Surviving Death* recounts the story of Atlas Aubrey, told by his mother Erica. She described how Atlas, at 1½ years old, began having nightmares during which his eyes would be open, and he would be screaming as if he was in pain. The doctors could not find any explanation and didn't know what to do. One evening at the age of 5, when they were driving home, Atlas said: "I miss when my mom took me to the playground." When Erica asked if he meant her, Atlas responded, "No, my other mom with the really pretty hair." He then told her that his name was Jaylen Robinson and his mom's name was Washington. He then said, "When I was this child, someone killed me" (*Surviving Death* 2021).

Erica didn't know where Atlas got those names, so she googled the name and found a news story about a 19-month-old boy who was murdered by his babysitter in Brooklyn, New York, in 2005. Erica and Atlas live in Evansville, Indiana. Erica contacted Dr Jim Tucker, a child psychiatrist at the University of Virginia School of Medicine, who specializes in researching cases of children who claim to have memories of past lives. Atlas was able to correctly identify for Tucker five photos from Jaylen's life, including the faces of Jaylen's mom and dad, their home, and several places the family would visit. Tucker said that Erica "could not have created that behavior in him, even if she was trying to make something up."

Atlas's past-life death story is that in March 2005, 40-year-old Tammy Williams was looking after 19-month-old Jaylen Robinson in her home while his parents, Kareen Washington and James Robinson, were working shiftwork and preparing to enroll him in a nearby daycare center. According to the *New York Times,* police were called to Williams' home in East New York at midnight on a Sunday in March. Jaylen, who was unconscious, was rushed to Brookdale University Hospital and Medical Center, where a short time later he was pronounced dead.

The death was considered a homicide by the medical examiner. The medical examiner stated that Jaylen had been smothered. It was reported that Jaylen had an ear infection and wouldn't stop crying, so Williams had placed duct tape over his mouth, before beating him and torturing him with a pair of scissors. She was charged with second-degree murder. On 11 June 2007, Williams took a plea deal and pleaded guilty to first-degree murder and was sentenced to 17 years in jail.

One of the most endearing stories of children remembering past lives is that of Jacqueline and Joanna Pollock. One morning in 1957, on their way to church in Hexham, England, both children, aged 4 and 6, were struck and killed by a car. About a year later, their mother, Florence Pollock, became pregnant again. Despite what the doctors said, John (their father) was certain that his wife was having twins and that they would be the reincarnated daughters that he had lost. Sure enough, nine months later, his prediction came true and twins Gillian and Jennifer were born.

When the twins were three months old, the family moved away from Hexham and didn't return for another four years. When the family did return, the twins began to name landmarks in their former town, and even the school that they said they had attended. They were able to accurately name all their deceased sisters' teddy bears and assorted dolls. One time when they saw a parked car, they became hysterical, saying that the car was coming for them. All these behaviors stopped around the age of 5, similar to the age at which their sisters had died. The Pollock family insists that they never told their twins anything about their dead sisters until they were older, claiming that the only explanation for these coincidences was reincarnation.

The practice of the search for and selection of "tulkus," or reincarnated lamas, in the Buddhist tradition is even more fascinating in the context of past-life remembrances and the continuation of consciousness. There are several tulku lineages in Tibetan Buddhism, including those of the Dalai Lama and the Karmapa. The selection of the reincarnated lama is often made from a written list of attributes left behind by the previous incarnation.

The movies *Unmistaken Child* (Unmistaken Child 2008) and *Tulku* (Tulku 2009) provide unique perspectives on the tulku tradition, highlighting its spiritual significance and personal challenges. *Unmistaken Child* follows Tibetan Buddhist monk Tenzin Zopa on his quest to find the reincarnation of his beloved teacher, Geshe Lama Konchog, who passed away in 2001. It offers an intimate look into the Tibetan tulku tradition and the emotional journey of those involved.

Tulku explores the fascinating lives of Western tulkus — individuals recognized as reincarnated Tibetan masters born outside the traditional Tibetan context. The movie delves into their struggles with identity, cultural expectations, and spiritual practice. It also features interviews with Dzongsar Rinpoche and examines how these tulkus navigate their roles in modern society.

While the ordinary person may not have such profound experiences as these reincarnated tulkus, consideration of your pre-life origin can prompt a deeper examination of the life you are now experiencing. Furthermore, the growing awareness of the significance of your current life here on Earth in the context of having lived many previous lives opens you to remember your true essence and nature, and to formulate a different outlook on death.

The issue of choosing our parents recounted in some of the examples is particularly noteworthy as it is not a widely accepted belief and takes reincarnation to another level. Yet this concept was accepted in many ancient cultures, including Buddhism, Hinduism, and some Native American beliefs. In choosing the experiences to have in this lifetime, one selects one from a range of options. Before incarnation, you may have asked certain members of your hereafter group to be your mother and father, or if you were looking for a particular experience, you may have had to ask several before you found someone who agreed to be your parent.

A common response to this concept is the question of why a child would choose a traumatic and difficult childhood. Yet, when considered in the context of many hundreds of lifetimes where the full gamut of all possible scenarios is experienced, it does not seem so unlikely that some of these will be lifetimes that appear difficult. The choice of an apparent traumatic childhood life is made from a higher spiritual perspective before incarnating.

Consideration of this higher spiritual perspective brings you to reflect on your origin even before you began incarnating in physical reality here on Earth. Contemplation of where you came from before you incarnated and the choices you made about this current life open the door to seeing your birth and subsequent death in a new and different light. As you become aware of your existence before this life, it gives credence to the existence of something after here. The pivotal place that death has in the greater cycle of life also starts to become clearer, and the consideration of what awaits you in the hereafter opens up the possibility of discovering some more interesting aspects of yourself.

Chapter 6

Who Were You?

Having experiences of past lives is quite common. Recognizing and understanding these experiences takes more consideration and analysis. The snippets of past lives that many people experience are frequently not recognized as such and are mostly ignored in Western societies. Despite personal experiences, the belief in reincarnation is often dismissed in today's materialistic world. Reincarnation is sometimes made fun of with stories of people who speak of being reincarnated kings or queens, or other important people. While we all can't have been Cleopatra or Napoleon, there are many accounts of people who have had previous lives, some of which are quite extraordinary.

Dorothy Eady is known for her belief that in a previous life she was a priestess in Ancient Egypt. Dorothy Eady was born in London in 1904. After falling down the stairs at the age of 3, her behavior appeared to change. At the British Museum in 1908, her parents first noticed Dorothy's strange behavior. Dorothy was obsessed with the Egyptian galleries and began kissing the feet of the statues. She sat down in front of a mummy enclosed in a glass case and did not want to be separated from it.

Dorothy had recurring dreams of columned buildings surrounded by beautiful gardens. When she came across photographs of Ancient Egypt, she showed her mother the hieroglyphics and remarked that she knew this language but had forgotten about it. When she saw a photo of the Temple of Seti I at Abydos, she ran to her father and proclaimed, "This is my home! This is where I used to live" (Psi Encyclopedia, no date).

Dorothy was obsessed with all things Egyptian and learned everything she could about Egyptology. In 1933, Dorothy married an Egyptian, Abdel Maguid, and went to live in Egypt. She called her son Seti, hence her new name "Omm Sety," meaning "Mother of Seti."

Eady's past-life story is that she lived in thirteenth-century BCE Egypt and was called Bentreshyt. She was raised in a temple, and after an affair with the young king Seti, she became pregnant and committed suicide to save Seti embarrassment.

In 1956, Omm Sety became the first woman to obtain a job in the Antiquities Department at Abydos, Egypt. While there, she was able to identify many previously unknown facts about the temple at Abydos. She identified a part that she said was a garden in her past life, and when excavated, ancient tree stumps were found there. She was reportedly able to touch particular scenes on a mural in the temple in total darkness. She also led archaeologists to a hidden tunnel at the north end of the temple. Omm Sety is known for having written 70 pages of hieroglyphics in an apparent trance state, which she said were dictated to her by "Hor-Ra," her spirit guide. Much of her information about her past life came in this way. Omm Sety's passion for everything Egyptian and her resolve to spend most of her life in Egypt point to something more profound than a simple fascination in this one lifetime.

The life story of Jenny Cockell is an incredible account of past-life remembrances. In 1989, Jenny Cockell traveled from her home in the UK to Malahide in County Dublin. In her book *Past Life, Future Life*, Cockell wrote, "I know I lived this previous life in Malahide in Dublin. I have always known it, and I have been telling people since I was three or four" (Cockell 1996). In her first book, *Yesterday's Children*, Jenny revealed the incredible search for her former family (Cockell 1993).

When Jenny was a child in North London in the 1950s, she was seeing images and having memories of a town where she once lived. She drew several pictures and maps of this town. While still a child, she opened an atlas at a map of Ireland and pinpointed the seaside town of Malahide in North County Dublin. As an adult in the 1980s, she began investigating her previous life. She compared her drawings to a map of the area from a bookshop and found that they matched exactly the east coast Irish town.

She went to Malahide in 1989 and walked through the town. She later recounted her thoughts: "It was like going back somewhere after 60 years — I noticed the changes. I went to the jetty and noticed it was now concrete when once it had been wood. The builder's yard on Church Street had gone and the railway station looked different" (IrishCentral, no date). Jenny also had memories of who she was in that previous life. She said that she was Mary Sutton, a mother of eight, from Malahide, and could recall many details of her final moments in Dublin's Rotunda Hospital in 1932.

Jenny searched out Mary Sutton's death certificate and then contacted her (Mary Sutton's) surviving children, Sonny, Phyllis, Betty, Frank, and Mary. She had nine pages of detailed notes that she shared with Sonny to be certain that the family she found was the family she was thinking of and worrying about. Sonny was convinced that she knew things only a relative could know.

In a meeting in 1990 with this older man she had given birth to in a previous life, she discovered that her memories matched everything she saw and remembered. Sonny agreed that she knew things only his mother could have known, and while they did not discuss reincarnation as an explanation at first, he felt that there was something strange going on. After meeting the other Irish children she gave birth to in her life as Mary Sutton, they accepted her. As reincarnation is contrary to some of their Catholic beliefs, they prefer to believe that their mother is working through her.

In Jenny's case, as with most well-known cases of past-life remembrances, there are both believers and those who are skeptical of the claims. Many people seem to remember a past life from an early age, while others recall memories while under hypnosis. The practice of hypnosis has been both a boon and a curse for those who seek to prove that reincarnation is a reality. Amazing information has come through past-life regression hypnosis for some people. On the other hand, the past-life regression of Jenny Cockell under hypnosis identified several pieces of information that did not tally with her life as Mary Sutton, while other pieces of information were quite accurate.

The benefits of past-life regression go further than simply remembering events from a previous life. It is not uncommon for a hypnotherapist treating a current life issue to ask a client to go back to the time and memory where the client's problem originated. Under such direction, the client often relates an experience from a former physical lifetime that is causing the present-day problem.

One of my firsthand experiences relates to a physical issue I had with my stomach for many years. At times, for no apparent reason, I would get a sharp pain in my stomach as if the muscles around my stomach suddenly got weaker. I remember on one occasion, when I was standing at a football match, not being able to stay standing because of the cramps in my stomach muscles, and I had to go and sit down elsewhere.

The first sense I got of this stomach issue changing was when I participated in a sweat lodge ceremony, which is a traditional Native American purification ritual akin to an extreme sauna with a spiritual healing and renewal aspect. At the end, as I crawled out of the sweat lodge, I threw myself on the ground and pressed the skin of my bare abdomen against the cold, refreshing ground. I felt an energy leave my stomach that was absorbed by the earth. I had a strong sense that this had something to do with my upcoming trip to Chartres, France, in a few weeks.

While waiting at the airport for my flight to Paris, I had a cup of tea with my now wife, Fionnuala. At one point, Fionnuala asked me if there was a soldier in my family, as she was psychically seeing someone in an army uniform in my energy field. I couldn't come up with any explanation that felt right to Fionnuala. Later, on the flight to France, I wrote in my journal as I contemplated who it might be:

> I recall a vivid dream I had several years ago in which I was a soldier running an explosive cable to destroy a building as the battle raged around me. I was and am now convinced that this was a past-life dream. Why it comes up now, I will find out in Chartres.

I could not sleep one night in Chartres, so I went for a walk at three in the morning. I walked along by the River Eure and out into the countryside. I walked for hours, always secure in the knowledge that I could see the floodlit cathedral on the hilltop in the distance and that it showed me my way back. Walking back into Chartres as I headed up the hill towards the cathedral, I passed a war memorial that contained hundreds of names from many different wars. I sat down on the plinth with my back to the memorial, but something caused me to turn around. As I looked at the lists of names, one name particularly caught my attention, as if it was rising up from the stone. I knew instantly that this was significant.

I took out my pendulum and began to ask questions about this name. The first question I asked was, "Was this me in a past life?" and I received a strong "Yes." I asked more questions and got more answers. I asked if I was shot and got a "Yes." I then started asking where I was shot: In the head? "No." In the chest? "No." In the stomach? As soon as I asked if I was shot in the stomach, my stomach went into severe spasms, and I was bent over double with the pain.

Once the pain had eased, I proceeded with my questions. I asked if I died on the battlefield, and I got a "No" response. Did

I die in a hospital? "No." I asked if I died in a farm shed, and I received a strong "Yes."

I told Fionnuala all about it on the phone that evening. She told me that on several occasions she had had a most vivid dream where she was a girl about 17 years old living on a farm during wartime. One day, a soldier crawled into the barn on the farm. He had been shot in the stomach. She held her hands over his stomach and tried to heal him, but he died.

Since the sweat lodge and my trip to Chartres, I have not had any trouble with my stomach. I believe that my past-life experience healed something in this lifetime. My connection with Fionnuala in that lifetime is also significant. Although it was only a fleeting few moments when she tried to heal me, the wounded soldier, I know that the reconnection is telling me that everyone in our life is important and has a meaningful role to play.

This story is a reminder to be open to the significance of every moment. Now I have a greater understanding and knowing of the interconnectedness of all of existence; that healing from past lives helps us in this life in physical, mental, emotional, and spiritual ways.

Chapter 7

Influences through Lifetimes

Reincarnation explains and clarifies much through the understanding of the continuity of life. Some of what people do today is a result of reincarnation. Love at first sight can be a remembrance of a deep relationship with a person in a past life. Natural aptitude and abilities in areas of art, music, and learning can all stem from a knowledge of the subject and practice in previous lives. If you find yourself drawn to a certain place, it may stem from having lived there in a past life. If you have a deep interest in some activity or period of history, then you may well have practiced that activity or lived at that time in a former life.

Some well-known historical figures may have drawn on past-life experiences in their work in their most recent life. The German poet Goethe was a master of 17 languages. The abilities of child prodigies could stem from past-life practice in that area. The Roman statesman, writer, and scholar Cicero wrote:

> It is again a strong proof of men knowing most things before birth, that when mere children they grasp innumerable facts with such speed as to show that they are not then taking them for the first time, but remembering and recalling them.
> (Tyrrell & Purser 1904–19)

Mozart composed his first piece when he was 5 years old. While Mozart's abilities may have been nurtured by his musician father, George Frideric Handel's father was opposed to any musical education and is said to have explicitly forbidden any musical instruments in the house. Handel was composing musical pieces by the age of 9.

The Chinese girl pianist Anke Chen, who wooed audiences in the USA when only 5 years old, could play Mozart, Bach, and Chopin, much of it from memory. French composer Camille Saint-Saens, at age 10, could play any of Mozart's piano concertos from memory. A consideration other than reincarnation is that children are more attuned to the nonphysical aspects of existence, and some may have an ability to tune into the universal consciousness where all information is stored and recreate intricate musical pieces as if from memory.

Plato believed in the transmigration of the soul from one lifetime to another, and in the reminiscence theory. According to Plato, we learn largely by anamnesis, the remembrance of things we knew before we were born into this world. We possess an innate knowledge, and learning consists of rediscovering that knowledge (Redfield, Murphy, & Timbers 2016). He considered that the soul stored knowledge during its lifetimes and that much of the learning in the current life is remembering what you already knew.

James Arthur Flowerdew from Norfolk in England claimed from about the age of 12 to have vivid visions and recollections of a great city carved in stone in the desert. These visions were particularly strong when he played with multicolored pebbles on a beach near his home. He laid out the pebbles in intricate patterns that he felt reflected the hues and textures of the great city's structures. One day, as an adult, he saw a BBC documentary on the ancient city of Petra in Jordan and recognized it as the city of his visions. Flowerdew's visions were so vivid that he felt as if he was almost living there. He even recounted being there as a soldier and being killed by a spear near the temple.

He contacted the BBC, who made a short piece on Flowerdew, after which he was questioned by an archaeologist who was an expert on Petra. The archaeologist came away perplexed by the depth of Flowerdew's knowledge of the city. He considered that Flowerdew could not have known all he did without serious archaeological research, even though Flowerdew insisted he had never even seen a book about Petra. Flowerdew came to the attention of the Jordanian Government, which brought him to Petra.

Flowerdew was able to comment in detail on the various landmarks in Petra and even identified sites that had yet to be excavated. He was able to explain the use of several items that had puzzled archaeologists. When he went into a military barracks, he pointed out the location of the guardroom and explained how the check-in system for the guards had worked, something that was unknown even to the experts. He even showed the place where an enemy had murdered him in the first century BCE. Flowerdew died in September 2002 at the age of 95.

The question of reincarnation is best approached from both a logical viewpoint and an intuitive perspective. Parents know that their child is born with a fully formed personality. Old people often state that they inwardly feel as they did when they were young. So, while the body might grow old, the essence of the person remains vibrant. The Ancient Greek philosopher Socrates considered that we must have received our knowledge of all realities before we were born, and that our souls formerly existed apart from our bodies and possessed intelligence before they came into human shape. Herbert Puryear, writing in *The Edgar Cayce Primer*, stated that "According to the readings, our emotional life comes primarily from previous Earth lives; the mental qualities come from experiences in other dimensions between incarnations" (Puryear 1982).

We remember past lives when we are ready to learn from the experiences and choose a different course of action in this lifetime. With every step you take on your journey of evolution, memories of your past lives will awaken, revealing the powerful patterns of growth and transformation you're creating. In the words of the Indian spiritual teacher Sivananda, "The past is veiled to you until it is helpful to remember it" (Sivananda 1946). Upon leaving the physical body, your spiritual self fully remembers all past lives and your time in the various realms of the hereafter. All aspects of you merge into the full wholeness of yourself.

If reincarnation exists, then there is also a reason, or reasons, for its existence. Many of the explanations for reincarnation indicate that the intention is to learn more and develop as a spiritual being. Because there is so much interconnectedness and a deep sense of oneness and shared consciousness in the Spirit World, it can be difficult to develop self-awareness. Therefore, taking form in a physical body in the lower and denser vibration of Earth brings a greater sense of separateness and individual independence. Life on Earth in the world of matter provides the resistance we need to awaken. All your life here on Earth is filled with opportunities to experience more, awaken, and remember who you really are.

Many famous people believed in reincarnation. Henry Ford, in an interview in the *San Francisco Examiner* on 26 August 1928, said that he adopted the theory of reincarnation when he was 26. He explained:

> Work is futile if we cannot utilize the experience we collect in one life in the next. When I discovered reincarnation, it was as if I had found a universal plan. I realized that there was a chance to work out my ideas. Time was no longer limited. I was no longer a slave to the hands of the clock.

Ford went on to say that:

> Genius is experience. Some seem to think that it is a gift or talent, but it is the fruit of long experience in many lives.

> Some are older souls than others, and so they know more. The discovery of reincarnation put my mind at ease. If you preserve a record of this conversation, write it so that it puts men's minds at ease. I would like to communicate to others the calmness that the long view of life gives to us.
> (Ford 1928)

The many arguments in favor of reincarnation include that the universal teaching of immortality demands it, and that it explains many mysterious experiences and extraordinary memories. Reincarnation alone solves the issue of apparent injustice and ill-fortune that seem to dominate many people's physical existence, as it takes an overview of all lives.

Reincarnation allows our awareness to move between existing in the expanded universal consciousness and the often-narrow confines of life in human form as we learn, grow, and evolve. In the words of Christopher Bache in his book *LSD and the Mind of the Universe*:

> Reincarnation gives individual consciousness an open-ended amount of time in which to learn from its mistakes and develop its innate capacities. Properly understood reincarnation is a work of genius, as is everything else we see in our universe, from supernovae to DNA.
> (Bache 2019)

Who you were in a previous existence can shed much light on your current life. I have found that most past-life experiences are opportunities to heal, learn, and advance in this current life. Such experiences arise for a reason, and the main reason is to find reconciliation and incorporate it into your current life. Yet who you are now is much more important than who you were. If you focus too much on the past for its own sake, then you may be missing some even more wonderful adventures in this lifetime. On the other hand, if you ignore prompts that point to a previous existence, you may also be missing out on some wonderful experiences in this life that have their roots in another life.

Chapter 8

Now Lives

All these past-life experiences are founded on the understanding that time is a fundamental part of our universe. Yet the concept that time does not exist is becoming increasingly prominent in fields such as spirituality, philosophy, and physics. It challenges our conventional understanding of reality as being time-based.

In Albert Einstein's theory of relativity, time is not an absolute fixed entity. In his theory, time is relative and dependent on the observer's frame of reference, especially concerning the speed of light. Time can slow down or speed up depending on factors such as velocity and gravity. This means that time is not the same for everyone and everywhere, leading some to consider that time is not a fundamental aspect of reality.

The "block universe" theory in physics, particularly when discussing spacetime, suggests that the past, present, and future all exist simultaneously. It suggests that our experience of time is just a human perspective, while reality itself is timeless. Past, present, and future all exist in a four-dimensional spacetime block.

Time is also a factor in the philosophical debate between presentism and eternalism. Presentism addresses whether only the present moment is real, while eternalism considers that past, present, and future all exist. Eternalism aligns with the block universe concept, suggesting that all points in time are equally real, while presentism asserts that only the "now" exists.

Philosophers such as Immanuel Kant have proposed that time (and space) are ways in which our mind structures experience, but they do not necessarily reflect the true nature of reality. Other philosophers argue that time is a product of human consciousness. According to this view, our minds impose the perception of time onto reality, creating the illusion of a past and a future, whereas in actuality only the present moment exists. The Irish philosopher George Berkeley considered that time is dependent on perception. He argued that the external world, including time, exists only as it is perceived by the mind.

The Eternal Now is a spiritual concept that time is an illusion and that the only true reality is the present moment. In Buddhist philosophy, time is often seen as a mental construct, and attachment to the past or future is considered a source of suffering. The core practice of mindfulness in both Theravada and Mahayana Buddhism emphasizes living in the present moment. Zen Buddhism similarly teaches the importance of living fully in the present. In his book *The Power of Now*, modern spiritual teacher Eckhart Tolle writes about living in the "Now" as a path to spiritual awakening, where past and future are seen as mental constructs rather than realities.

So, rather than having past lives, all your experiences can be considered to be "now lives." Each "now life" is like a stream of information that flows separately from the others. Your different lifestreams are all happening at the same time. Some are past lives, some are future lives, and some are lives happening in other galaxies and dimensions. You are mostly not aware of these other lifestreams as your primary focus is on the life you are currently living.

Having more than one "lifestream" is a result of the actions of your "infinite self." Your infinite self is the greatest version of you that exists in multidimensional consciousness. It is the source of individual consciousness in the greater consciousness that exists beyond time and space. Your infinite self decides to have different experiences in different dimensions and perceived different times on Earth, all at the same time. Your primary focus in your current state of consciousness is on the present experiences that you are having in this lifetime. However, you are also having other life experiences in different times and dimensions. The infinite self is the higher consciousness that you gain access to in deep meditation and altered states. It can act as a guide in this reality and can create synchronicities as it has full knowledge of all aspects of the choices you made for this current lifetime.

When your lifelines overlap, or when one of these other lifelines briefly crosses into this lifetime, you have the experience of a past life. The sense of déjà vu that you sometimes experience is because of two lifelines coming together simultaneously, causing you to know more about, or be more familiar with, a place or people than if you were only experiencing it in one lifetime. Similarly, the feeling that you know someone on a deep level, even when only having met them briefly, is indicative of you both having experiences together in more than one lifetime. The concept of overlapping now lives may also explain such phenomena as child prodigies, inexplicable talents, phobias, advanced IQ, mastery of unknown languages, and even transgender orientation.

Regardless of how you view time in relation to your current and other lives, if you have an experience of death in another life it can be either beneficial or unhelpful, depending on your remembered experience. When you remember a previous death, it is usually to heal any wounds that you are carrying in this life around death. Your remembering is happening so that you address all aspects of it and move into a more peaceful and loving approach to your forthcoming death in this life.

Soul

In considering who you were, it is even more important to explore the question of who you are now. We have already considered that you are not your physical body. Who or what you are other than your physical body involves looking further into the concept of the soul.

The soul is an abstract concept that seeks to define the essence of what makes you unique. It is frequently seen as the core of your being, representing your true self, personality, consciousness, or your spiritual aspect. It is usually considered eternal, persisting beyond physical death. This belief underpins ideas of reincarnation, the hereafter, and spiritual transcendence.

The soul is frequently believed to be connected to, or part of, a divine or cosmic source. In some traditions, it is seen as a fragment of a universal spirit or created by a higher power. The soul is also frequently associated with a person's morality, character, and spiritual growth. It is seen as something that can be nurtured, corrupted, or redeemed based on one's actions and choices.

The concept of having a soul, or being a soul, is separation thinking. It can cause confusion as to who and what you are. Consideration of whether you have a soul or are a soul gives rise to questions about what your soul exactly is. Lack of clarity about the soul can keep you from realizing your infinite self. The soul is a limited description of the consciousness that you are.

The soul, oversoul, and higher self are concepts that generally apply to one individual lifestream. They usually do not take into account the many lives you are experiencing at the same time. The infinite self, on the other hand, is the whole of you that exists in many realms and dimensions simultaneously.

Your current existence is an aspect of your infinite self that is projecting a part of its consciousness into this lifestream. In this life, it has chosen not to be initially aware of itself but rather to experience the unfolding of events and evolve through choosing how to respond to each situation as it arises. Experiences from all your lives are accumulated by the infinite self upon the death of the physical aspect of you in each particular life. The infinite you evolves through all the experiences that it is having.

Creation

Regardless of whether you consider that you are a soul, oversoul, higher self, or infinite self, the question of where you come from remains. Where, how, and when you were created are perennial questions that have occupied the minds of philosophers, theologians, scientists, and spiritual teachers for millennia. These questions remain largely unanswered. Yet, in moving to a state of loving death, considering the origin of your existence helps to inform and even change your approach to death.

Regardless of what creation theory you believe in, or if you believe in none of them, it appears that there is something from which all of creation emerged. Creation theories found in the Bible, the Quran, Hindu texts, and other cosmologies all point to the existence of something to bring about the creation of the universe as we know it.

One of the most widely accepted scientific explanations for the universe's origin is the Big Bang theory. It posits that around 13.8 billion years ago, all matter and energy were concentrated in a singularity, which then expanded rapidly. This led to the formation of space, time, and eventually stars, galaxies, and planets. Yet the biggest question that remains in this theory is what existed before the Big Bang, or what caused the Big Bang to happen. Logic dictates that there must have been something there before the Big Bang, rather than it just happening by itself out of nothing.

In other words, something always existed. Names given to this something include God, Spirit, the Tao, and the Universe. Western religions tend to personify God, while Eastern philosophies such as Buddhism are focused more on enlightenment and understanding the nature of suffering. Taoism teaches that the Tao is an eternal, natural order that flows through all things and is not specifically a god but rather an essence or force. Whatever name you choose to put on this energy, if something always existed, and you are part of this something, then you always existed. You are an infinite, immortal being.

As regards the creation of this reality that we call Earth, there is a growing interest in and support for simulation theory, particularly with the rise in computer technology and virtual realities, and how they work. In simulation theory, this reality you are experiencing here on Earth is considered to be a complex simulation, with its creators controlling or monitoring its development.

One of the leading proponents of simulation theory is Tom Campbell, who believes that this physical reality is a sophisticated virtual reality or simulation. Campbell worked as a physicist in technology development and complex-system risk analysis for both government and industry. In addition, for over 50 years he explored scientific, drug-free research into altered states of consciousness. This unique combination enabled him to develop My Big TOE (Theory of Everything), a scientific model of reality based on the insight that consciousness, and not matter, is fundamental to all existence.

Tom Campbell's theory on consciousness centers on two main principles: that consciousness is the foundation of reality, and that evolution drives its progression. He believes that a larger, nonphysical consciousness, termed the "Larger Consciousness System" (LCS), is the source of all existence, with physical reality just one of many "virtual realities" within it (Campbell 2003).

Campbell's second principle is that evolution directs the development of consciousness towards lower entropy, which means greater organization, understanding, and efficiency. According to him, consciousness evolves by growing through experiences, learning, and love, and by reducing entropy within itself and the larger system.

In this framework, life's purpose is to evolve consciousness and reduce entropy through choices and actions that emphasize growth and compassion. Death is viewed as a transition that enables further evolution, freeing consciousness from physical limitations and allowing it to continue learning in nonphysical forms. Reincarnation, in this view, retains not memories but the quality of consciousness, shaping future experiences.

This perspective encourages people to transcend the fear of death and live meaningfully, focusing on love and connection to contribute to the evolution of the Larger Consciousness System. The love of life leads to reduced entropy, and the love of death leads to even greater reductions in entropy as it not only reduces the fear of death but also contributes to reducing fear in general.

Chapter 9

Way to Go

There is no greater satisfaction than a job well done. The expression "way to go" shows pleasure, approval, or excitement. It is a form of congratulations, and a new way to look at death. When I leave my body, please shout to the heavens, "Way to go, Tony!" I will hear you and smile as you celebrate my death.

When your thoughts turn to your death, you most likely do not know how it will happen. People have different views and wishes about how they would like to die. Some may say that they are not afraid of the moment of death but that they do not want the physical process of dying to be painful and drawn out. How you see, and especially feel about, your dying and death will have a bearing on them. Your thoughts and feelings are powerful manifesters and can help bring about whatever you choose to feel and think.

French medical doctor Jean-Jacques Charbonier gathered information on common experiences from his observations of patients on the point of dying. He found that the most common states of being of the dying were of calm resignation when faced with the imminence of death, followed by feelings of serenity and inner peace. Further common experiences were heightened spirituality with invocation of divinities and the recital of prayers. Also, a sense of euphoria and curiosity at the idea of discovering a hereafter were all more common than anguish and fear at the idea of dying or a terror that is hard to control (Charbonier 2012).

Nobody dies without giving permission. Your infinite self has already decided on your exit plans. At the appointed and chosen time, the aspect of the consciousness of the infinite self that you now are decides to leave the physical body and gives permission for the body to die.

You can choose how you die. You have already chosen, although you most likely do not remember. Before you came to Earth to occupy a physical body during your life-planning stage, you chose several ways to leave the body. You may already have experienced one or more of these opportunities but chose not to take them. It is not uncommon to hear about someone who walked away unscathed from a serious car crash, or to occasionally hear of someone who was delayed and missed a flight that subsequently crashed, or someone who had a miraculous recovery from a serious illness.

How you now choose to die most likely reflects one of the options that you have chosen. Depending on how well life is progressing, you may choose a predetermined exit point, or you may decide to change a preplanned exit. However, if the ego becomes over-dominant and takes over the act of deliberately ending your physical life, that goes against the options for death that you gave yourself before you incarnated. Suicide is rarely a chosen option from the viewpoint of your infinite self, as one of the main reasons for incarnating is to have experiences that guide your evolution. Suicide goes against this principle, and while your physical body may be no more, your emotional state stays with you in the hereafter. You will still have to deal with your emotional state but without the benefits of having a physical body to work with.

You regularly receive notice of your impending death. The death of others serves as a reminder of the shortness of human life. Each death you hear of is an opportunity to consider your death. Most do not consciously choose to do this and instead choose subconsciously to enter into the emotions and drama of the loss of the deceased person.

Now is the time to prepare for death. You can practice how you might like to be at your death by seeing how you are at the death of friends and family members. With deeper personal and spiritual preparation, your awareness of how you want to depart this life and body becomes clearer.

Small everyday happenings are also reminders of your impending death. The appearance of your first gray hair or your receding hairline are wonderful reminders of the aging of the body. Wrinkles on your skin, losing some of your teeth, hearing loss, and reduced body strength and stamina are all prompts for contemplating the decline of the physical body, and its ultimate demise.

Obvious signs of the aging human body are usually considered negative. Great efforts are made to find ways of covering them up. Hair implants, facelifts, hair dye, anti-wrinkle cream, and a host of other products and procedures are used to mask the appearance of the decline of the physical body. There are collective thought-forms of fear, anxiety, and negativity around aging. These collective emotions form an "accepted" reality that is so strong that one individual may not be able to transcend it and create their own thoughts and emotions about life, aging, and death.

Because the predominant human consciousness involves attachment to the physical body, death is viewed mostly in the context of the dying process rather than the moment of death itself. Death is simply the separation of your consciousness from the physical body and the physical realm. There is no pain or unpleasant experience involved in your actual death. It is not fearful or mysterious unless you continue to allow yourself to think it is so.

Death Mastery

Some people have transcended the common thinking and beliefs around death. There are even those who have achieved what appears to be mastery over death. Numerous holy individuals, yogis, and other spiritually advanced beings have not only been aware of their impending death but have even chosen the time and means of their death.

Some advanced yogis are said to have achieved the state of *mahasamadhi* — the conscious and intentional departure from the physical body by a realized yogi or spiritual master at the time of their death, signifying their union with the divine. It is generally only possible when they have already realized the state of *nirvikalpa samadhi*, an enlightened state with minimal contact with the body.

Lahiri Mahasaya was an Indian yogi and a disciple of Mahavatar Babaji, from whom he learned the practice of Kriya Yoga. He helped spread Kriya Yoga throughout the world through his disciples, such as Sri Yukteswar Giri, who was the guru of the renowned Paramahansa Yogananda.

In 1895, Lahiri Mahasaya began letting some of his disciples know that he would soon be leaving the body. For hours, he spoke about the Bhagavad Gita, and then moments before his passing he said simply, "I am going home. Be comforted; I shall rise again." He then stood up, turned his body around three times, faced north, and consciously left his body, entering *mahasamadhi* (Yogananda 1946). Lahiri Mahasaya died on 26 September 1895.

At the age of 63, Zen master Tung-shan (or Dongshan Liangjie), announced to his disciples in the year 869 that he was going to leave his body. He took a bath, shaved his head, put on his robe, gathered his disciples, and sat in meditation. It appeared to all that he had died, whereupon his disciples cried loudly. Tung-shan opened his eyes and rebuked his followers by saying that monks and followers of Buddha Dharma are meant to be detached from all things external and transitory. He said that self-cultivation means to live is to work, to die is to rest. What is the use of moaning and grieving? He then ordered that a meal to ignorance, a delusion banquet, be prepared. After a week of preparation he ate sparingly of the meal, bade his disciples farewell, saying not to fuss over him or make a great commotion over nothing, went to his room, and died (Ferguson 2011).

The Swedish scientist, philosopher, and mystic Emanuel Swedenborg (1688–1772) predicted the exact time of his death with a calm confidence that was in line with his deep spiritual beliefs. In the final days of his life in early March 1772, while staying in London, Swedenborg began telling those close to him that his death was imminent and specified the time and date he would pass.

In the book *Memoirs of Swedenborg's Life,* written around 1782, Carl Robsahm, who had known Swedenborg personally, compiled accounts of his interactions and observations of Swedenborg, including anecdotes about Swedenborg's predictions of his own death. Swedenborg passed away precisely when he had predicted, around 5 p.m. on 29 March 1772. He remained composed and spiritually centered, showing no fear or distress as the time approached (Robsahm 2011).

Swedenborg's announcement of his death aligned with his unique beliefs and experiences regarding the spiritual world. He held that life after death was merely a continuation of one's earthly existence on a spiritual plane, and he claimed to have visited these realms frequently. For Swedenborg, the soul's journey was an ongoing process of spiritual growth and self-realization, which contributed to his serene approach to the end of his physical life.

While the revered Indian sage Ramana Maharshi did not explicitly predict the date of his death, he demonstrated profound acceptance and awareness of his impending passing due to sarcoma. He taught "Self-enquiry" ("Who am I?") as the most direct path to realizing the eternal Self, emphasizing that true peace lies in transcending the ego and recognizing one's innate awareness. As he neared his death, he assured devotees that his presence would remain eternal, stating: "Where can I go? I am here." He remained calm and composed as he approached his final moments. His serene departure on 14 April 1950 was marked by a meteor-like light seen over Arunachala Hill, interpreted as symbolic of his spiritual transcendence.

These and other great spiritual masters knew much more than the everyday person about death and their life force. When even just one person can achieve a level of mastery over the death of the physical body and their interconnected life force, that ability is then in the consciousness of humanity and may be attained by anyone who sincerely seeks it. While you may not be able to choose the means of the death of the body, you can prepare for and choose your state of mind and being at the moment of death. In this way, you are choosing your way to go.

Chapter 10

Dissolution of the Body at Death

In choosing your way to go, learning about the decreasing functioning of the body and mind as death approaches also prepares you for when your time to depart nears. Mystical traditions talk about the dissolution of the elements in the dying process. It is a concept found in the Eastern philosophies of Tibetan Buddhism and Hinduism. It is also found in the Celtic tradition as described by Phyllida Anam-Áire in her book *The Last Ecstasy of Life: Celtic Mysteries of Death and Dying* (Anam-Áire 2021), and in Gnostic Christian mysticism as detailed by Tau Malachi in his book *Gnosis of the Cosmic Christ* (Malachi 2005).

The dissolution of the elements describes the progressive breakdown of the body's elements (earth, water, fire, air, and ether or space) as one moves through the stages of dying. These elements are associated with different physical and mental processes that gradually cease functioning as death nears. Progression through the dissolution of the elements is mostly linear. The most common progression through the elements is from earth (form) to water (feeling), to fire (perception), to air (intellect), then ether or spirit-space (consciousness), although Phyllida Anam-Áire has the progression from earth to fire, then to water and air.

The first element that noticeably begins to dissolve is the earth element. Physical signs are of the body losing its strength; muscles weaken, and you may feel heavy or unable to support your own body. Your perception may be a sinking feeling, or that the bedclothes feel uncomfortably heavy as a sense of pressure and weight builds up. The focus of your mind shifts from the external world, and concentration wanes. You may inwardly see visions of shimmering mirages, and images of those who have already died.

Water is the next element to start dissolving. Physical signs may be the sensation of fluids leaving the body, then the bodily fluids drying up. The mouth, throat, and eyes become dry, and the ability to produce saliva or tears diminishes. The digestion and urinary processes slow down or stop. Emotions tend to diminish, and you may feel detached or cold as the flow of life is draining away. You might see inwardly visions of wisps of mist-like substances, like smoke rising from an incense stick.

The fire element dissolution is indicated by the decrease in the body's temperature, as all warmth moves from the extremities to the heart. Your feet may feel cold, and your digestive "fire" weakens, making it difficult to metabolize food. Your body's energy weakens, and you become feebler. Mental clarity begins to fade, and your thoughts may become confused or hazy. Your vision may dim, and memory also starts to dissolve as the warmth of life fades. Some inwardly see sparks of fire as if rising from a campfire.

The air element is primarily related to the breath. As air dissolves into spirit-space, your breathing becomes irregular, shallow, or labored. Your inhalations become increasingly shorter and your exhalations increasingly longer. The body is no longer able to regulate breathing, and the respiratory system starts to collapse. A feeling of airlessness or suffocation may occur, with a sense of breathing out for the last time. Thoughts become erratic or completely cease, and consciousness begins to withdraw from the external reality. You may begin to see visions, which may be fearful or peaceful, reflecting how you have lived your life. As you take your final breath, it marks the end of your physical existence.

The ether element is mainly associated with the mental and emotional space of your awareness rather than the physical body. As the connection to the bodily functions dissolves, there is a complete withdrawal of awareness from the senses. Your attention turns inwards as all physical sensations and thoughts cease. This is the point where perception of the physical world dissolves, leaving you in a state of pure consciousness.

These stages are seen in Buddhist teachings as the path the body and mind take as they prepare for death. They lead to the clear light of death, which is the state of pure awareness or consciousness free from any material form. In Hinduism, this process can be considered to be the process of the *atman* (soul) preparing to leave the body and move towards rebirth or liberation (*moksha*).

In the Gnostic mystical approach, Tau Malachi sees death and dying as a process of the dissolution of the gross and subtle elements of consciousness into the primordial nature of consciousness. He considers that death can be a vehicle of self-realization through an understanding of the process and spiritual practice, and that for the Gnostic initiate, death presents a wonderful opportunity and is viewed as the final adventure that life offers.

Notwithstanding this description of the dissolution of the elements, there are other accounts of the death of the body that appear magical to the uninitiated. In the Buddhist Dzogchen tradition, there is a practice known as the rainbow body, where a fully accomplished practitioner can dissolve their body at the time of death. In this practice, the body becomes smaller and smaller until it dissolves, emitting a rainbow light, until finally only the hair and nails are left behind.

A widely witnessed instance of the rainbow body was recorded in the east of Tibet in 1952. Sonam Namgyal was a humble man who was an itinerant stone-carver of mantras and sacred texts. He did not openly practice and was known as a "hidden yogin." Just before his death at the age of 79, he made a request for when he died: "Don't move my body for a week." When he died, his family wrapped his body and invited monks and lamas to come and practice religious rituals for him. As they were placing his body in a small room, they noticed that his body had become smaller. At this time, an extraordinary rainbow-colored light was seen all around the house. On the sixth day, when they looked into the small room, they noticed that the body was becoming smaller and smaller. On the morning of his funeral, eight days after his death, when the undertakers came to collect the body, they found only nails and hair under the coverings (Blackman 1997).

There have been many instances of visual evidence of something leaving the physical body at death. In a study conducted by Jean-Jacques Charbonier on perceptions connected to death, he found that in 31 of the 42 case studies there were visual perceptions by onlookers of smoke, fog, vaporous silhouettes moving out of the body, or luminous shapes more or less well-defined (Charbonier 2012).

Just as spiritual masters knew when their time was coming close, so can you. As you become more aware of your spiritual energy and live in a constant state of connection to it, you are well on your way to knowing when it is your time to leave the body and how you choose to leave. Most of the spiritual masters already mentioned leave in a way that they have practiced during their spiritual journey. This is often some form of meditation or a discipline that involves temporarily moving energetically outside the physical body.

The act of living as a spiritual being in a physical body amplifies your understanding of all things energetic, spiritual, and physical. You no longer have unbreakable ties to the physical. You see everything as spiritual and your time here on Earth as part of your spiritual journey. When you have fulfilled what you came here to do, and experienced all that you came to experience, then you are ready to leave.

There are rituals and meditation practices in many traditions to assist the dying person in this transition. Depending on your beliefs, you can choose to study one or more of these or create your own. The process of dying is not something to fear but is to be seen as a sacred transformation where you return to unite with the creative energy of all that is. Seen in this way, your death is a passage to higher, more enlightened states of being in the presence of infinite, unconditional love. Death – you gotta love it.

Chapter 11

You'll Never Die Alone

Dying alone does not happen. Your loved ones who have already crossed over, angels, and guides are all there with you. Your guides are spiritual workers who have been assisting you in the background throughout your life. They have usually finished their incarnations in the physical plane and are now helping others during their time on Earth. Just as they have helped you during your life, they are waiting for you and supporting you as you transition.

If you die in old age or after a long illness, you will most likely have drifted between the physical earthly world and the Spirit World several times before you finally cross over. This moving back and forth helps you to become accustomed to the different energy and ways of being in the Spirit World. The energy in the Spirit World is lighter and of a higher vibration, so checking it out for periods before you transition helps you to become acquainted with what will be your new (or old) familiar surroundings.

In the days before they cross over, many people talk about seeing their loved ones who have already passed. Near the transition, people can appear to drift in and out of consciousness, sleeping a lot and waking for brief moments. This is part of the preparation for letting go of the physical body. In those waking moments when the dying person talks of seeing family and loved ones who have already passed, do not dismiss this. If possible, acknowledge that they are looking through a doorway into the next realm and will soon be joining them. If they can talk, ask them about what they see and how they feel about seeing them. They may even feel excited about where they will shortly be going and who they will be reunited with.

Deathbed visions are visions experienced by the dying that appear quite clear to the person experiencing them. Common characteristics include the person staring straight ahead with a fixed gaze on something or someone that they are pleased to meet but that most others cannot see. They appear happy and become calm and peaceful. Thereafter, any pain or distress of dying dissipates, enabling the person to pass in peace.

One widely witnessed deathbed vision account is found in the 1926 book *Death-Bed Visions* by Sir William Barrett, a professor of physics at the Royal College of Science in Dublin. Barrett's wife, Lady Florence Barrett, a prominent gynecologist and obstetrician, and Dean of the London School of Medicine for Women, details how one of her patients, known as "Mrs B" in the records, was dying due to heart failure after the birth of her baby. The most important evidence was given by Miriam Castle, the matron (head nurse) of the hospital.

Doris, the dying lady, started speaking the words "Lovely, lovely," and when asked by Lady Barrett what was lovely, she replied, "What I see — lovely brightness, wonderful beings." Then, looking at one particular place in the room, she said, "Why, it's Father. Oh, he's so glad I'm coming. I can see Father; he wants me, he is lonely, I am coming." She then said, in a rather puzzled way, "He has Vida with him." Vida was the dying woman's sister who had passed away about two weeks earlier, but Doris had not been informed of her passing due to her own serious condition.

This case was also witnessed by the hospital's resident medical officer and by the dying woman's mother. In this case, as in many other recorded cases of people experiencing deathbed visions, Doris was lucid, rational, and aware of her surroundings when the visions were taking place. At one point, she gently pushed her husband aside, saying, "Won't you let me see the lovely brightness?" Lady Florence Barrett observed that Doris "appeared to have retained to the last the double consciousness of the bright forms she saw, and also of those tending her at her bedside" (Barrett 1926).

After Sir William Barrett's death in 1925, his wife Florence, initially skeptical of mediumship, became convinced of its authenticity after numerous sittings with renowned trance medium Gladys Osborne Leonard. Some key aspects of these communications were that Sir William provided intimate details known only to Florence, and made factual statements later verified as correct. Sir William also shared profound thoughts about the nature of life and existence, emphasizing that life does not reside in the physical body but in an "etheric" medium. He described the etheric body as a carrier of life energy distinct from the physical (Barrett & Barrett 2020).

A similar account of a near-death vision in which the person became aware of new information through their vision is found in the 1993 book *Final Gifts* by Maggie Callanan. She wrote about an elderly Chinese woman who had a death vision in which she saw her deceased husband and her sister. She was puzzled since her sister wasn't dead, or so she thought. In actuality, her family had hidden her sister's recent death from her for fear of upsetting her already fragile health (Callanan & Kelley 2012).

It is common for people near death to be seen talking to an apparently invisible person. Irish author Colm Keane has written several books about stories from the edge of death. With the move from a home setting to a hospital for many near death, deathbed experiences are now more likely to be experienced by hospital staff than family and friends at home.

Keane has many deathbed vision stories in his book *We'll Meet Again: Irish Deathbed Visions: Who You Meet When You Die*. One such account is given by Sean, a priest from Tipperary, at the death of his father in 2012. His father had been unwell for a while and had come home for his last few days, but he held on for a few weeks. One day near his end, Sean's father asked him to say Mass. All the family was there, and then his father appeared to become agitated. He was quite weak, sitting propped up with pillows, and indicated that he wanted everyone to pray, and Sean felt: "This is it."

Then Sean's father put his hand out to his wife, Sean's mother, and shook her hand, saying, "I wish you a long life after I go." He then shook hands with everyone there. But then his hands came up again and he seemed to grasp and shake hands with what to Sean was an open space, while smiling and looking happy. Nobody there really knew what was going on. Then Sean's father had his two hands out and was embracing whoever he was meeting. Some were getting handshakes and others were getting hugs. Sean was convinced that there were more people in the room than he could see, but his father was able to see them. His father died the following day (Keane 2017).

These deathbed visions appear quite genuine and convincing, and they seem to bring a sense of surprise and astonishment to the dying while also being comforting and calming. If the deceased appear to those near death, it adds further evidence for the existence of a hereafter, especially in cases such as that of Doris and the Chinese lady, who both received visitations from their sisters who, unknown to them, had already died.

Dr James L. Hallenbeck, Director of Palliative Care Services with the Veterans Administration Palo Alto Health Care System, estimates that pre-death visions or deathbed visions of deceased loved ones occur prior to at least 25 percent of deaths (Hogan 2020). In their book *At the Hour of Death*, Karlis Osis and Erlendur Haraldsson published their research into extensive interviews with over 1000 doctors and nurses in the USA and India who were present when cases of "post-mortem existence" occurred. They concluded, based on the information given by the nurses and physicians they interviewed, that "The majority of the patients who had these visionary experiences were in a normal, wakeful state of consciousness" (Osis & Haraldsson 2012). In other research by Osis and Haraldsson, their study concluded that deathbed visions are a reasonable indicator of imminent death. Over one-quarter of those experiencing them die within an hour of the vision, while the majority die within one day.

Elsewhere in his research, Osis made the significant finding that fear is not a dominant emotion in most dying patients. He found that while discomfort and pain were more common, what was surprising was the large number of patients who were elated or had a sense of euphoria reported near the time of their death. Patients experiencing this often appeared content and expressed feelings of fulfillment or readiness to pass on.

Deathbed visions have also been mentioned in sacred scriptures of some religions. In the Zohar, the chief text of the Jewish Kabbalah, it is written that:

> At the hour of a man's departure from this world, his father and relatives gather round him, and he sees them and recognizes them, and likewise all with whom he associated in this world, they accompany his soul to the place where it is to abide.
> (Zohar 1:217b)

When one considers the possible meaning and significance of deathbed visions, it is difficult to dismiss the evidence that those who have already died appear to the dying. The peace that such visions bring to many people near death has been witnessed innumerable times by family members, friends, nurses, and carers. Where death might have once seemed like a frightening experience, the appearance of a deceased loved one to the dying person makes the transition to their next state of being easier and even joyful. Overall, deathbed visions appear to be peaceful and highly positive experiences, preparing the dying for their transition by raising their consciousness and awareness, helping them tune into the dimensions of the hereafter.

The phenomenon of deathbed visions leads one to consider that at the moment of death, there appears to be an opening between dimensions, or a coming together or convergence and intrusion of one into the other. The transition from one dimension into another can also be seen in the tunnel of light that many having a death experience talk about. It sounds very similar to the wormhole-type effect that is postulated as a way of moving between dimensions.

Be aware that if you believe that there will be no one there to meet and assist you when you die, then you may unintentionally block those who are there to help you. Your guides and helpers will be trying to get your attention, so stay alert as best you can to what might be happening around you.

You will be peaceful when you die. Whatever worries, fears, or restlessness you might be carrying with you dissolve in your final moments in this dimension. Hypnotherapist Michael Newton writes in his book *Journey of Souls* that:

> Although there are dying people who find acceptance to be more difficult than resignation, caregivers working around the dying say most everyone acquires a peaceful detachment near the end. I believe dying people are given access to a supreme knowledge of eternal consciousness, and this frequently shows in their faces. Many of these people realize something universal is out there waiting, and it will be good.
> (Newton 1994)

So, rather than fearing death, the knowledge that you will not be alone, and that you will be meeting already deceased loved ones in a beautiful place, is a reassurance that you too will find peace as you die and learn to love that moment of transition called "death."

Chapter 12

Enjoy the Ride

Buckle up and enjoy the ride through the exhilarating journey of death! The journey through death to your next level of existence has been comprehensively and repeatedly documented. The hundreds of thousands of death-experience accounts have consistently similar details of what to expect when you leave the body.

Death experiences are experiences that people have when they have clinically died, usually at the time of a major accident or operation, and later come back to life. Some of these experiences are short-lived, and others can last a considerable amount of time. While one such account could be dismissed as hallucination or dreaming, when taken together, the body of evidence from these accounts overwhelmingly points to an existence beyond this one in which we now live.

The term "near-death experience" or NDE was first coined by Raymond Moody in his book *Life After Life*. Moody, a physician, psychologist, and author, analyzed 150 accounts of people who had near-death experiences and interviewed around 50 people who had survived clinical death (Moody 1975). The results of the study showed great similarities and common experiences in the reports of the subjects. He sparked much interest, inspired further research, and received widespread media coverage. A Gallup poll carried out in the USA in 1980 showed that about eight million people living in the USA at the time reported having near-death experiences (Gallup 1982). Dutch cardiologist Pim van Lommel studied 344 cases of patients with cardiac arrest in ten Dutch hospitals and found that 18 percent of them recounted near-death experiences (Van Lommel et al. 2001). In children who were close to death, more than 50 percent reported similar experiences.

When one considers the evidence relating to what Moody called "near-death experiences," they appear to be experiences of death from which a person returns. They could be more accurately described as "death experiences," as this lends more weight to our understanding of death and helps inform our own forthcoming death experience, from which we will not return to our current body.

A typical death experience involves floating above the physical body, feeling calm and peaceful, and looking down on the body and the scenes around it. Sometimes there is a sense of being in a void, then traveling at speed through a tunnel of light, spending time in a beautiful otherworldly realm, meeting deceased relatives and beings of light, and returning, sometimes reluctantly, to one's own body. Many NDEs also involve a life review where you re-enact your current life as it was experienced and felt by the other people in your life. The overall feeling is one of immense and total love, and an absence of judgment by others.

In most death experiences, the person having the experience knows beyond any doubt that life exists after death. Many say that it feels more real than life here in the physical realm. The level of consciousness and awareness during a death experience appears to be higher than in everyday life, even though these experiences usually occur when the person is clinically dead or unconscious.

Many of those who return experience significant life changes. They feel different than before their death experience and have a renewed sense of purpose in how they choose to live their lives. They often have a newfound energy for life and a desire to lead a more meaningful and fulfilling existence. An increased awareness of the beauty of creation and humanity is common, and many develop a growing interest in spiritual matters. They have greater compassion for all of life and a desire to make the world a better place. The transformative effect on the person often includes losing the fear of death.

The profound life changes that occur after a death experience happen not only to the person themselves but also to those they live with. Jim Bruton, recounting his death experience in the series *The In Between*, said on the Gaia platform that there is a 70 percent divorce rate among people who have had NDEs (*The In Between with Jim Bruton* 2021).

One of the oldest accounts of a death experience in Western literature is found in Plato's *Republic*, written in 380 BCE. Plato wrote about the Myth of Er, a soldier who was killed in battle. When the bodies of those who had died were being collected, Er's body was still undecomposed. Two days later, he revived on his funeral pyre and told of his journey in the hereafter.

Er's journey is remarkably similar to some aspects of modern-day death experiences. He leaves the body and travels to the hereafter, where there is a judgment of deeds that determines the final destination. The hereafter is a place of great beauty where he meets loved ones long dead. Plato goes on to say that you choose a next life different from your previous one in character, and usually directly contrasting and relating to the life just lived. Once rebirth is imminent, you must drink from the Lethe, the river of forgetfulness, so that you are born without knowledge of the eternal nature of who you are and your previous lifetimes.

One extraordinary death-experience account comes from Dannion Brinkley. In his book *Saved by the Light*, he recounts his experiences during the 28 minutes he was clinically dead, and his amazing life afterwards. Brinkley had not one death experience but two. He died after being struck by lightning and saw his own dead body twice — when he left it and when he returned (Brinkley 1994).

During his death experience, Brinkley was brought to the Spirit World and welcomed by a powerful and loving being with whom he saw his whole life review. He was taken to a beautiful crystal city where he met 13 "light beings" who filled him with knowledge. He was then shown boxes with video images of things happening that he did not understand. Upon returning to his body, and as time passed, he realized that these boxes contained visions of the future. While he had his first death experience in 1975, he was shown significant world events such as the breakup of the Soviet Union in 1989, the Gulf War of 1990, and other major world events.

When Brinkley returned to his body, he was in very poor health. It took years for him to return to any sense of normality. His pain was so great that he wanted to die, and he had no fear of dying. He wrote that he was "doomed to live," as that was how he felt about going on (Brinkley 1994).

The experience where the person rises above their body and observes attempts to save or resuscitate them is a relatively common occurrence. In several of these verified accounts, there is no way that the scene could have been observed if the consciousness was still in the body and the experience generated solely by brain activity. It would appear, then, that while some aspects of death experiences can be similar to hallucinatory physiological brain activity, what is happening in death experiences is more than just that.

There are even cases of people who were blind being able to see when they rose above their body, and upon returning to their body, no longer being able to see again. Kenneth Ring and Sharon Cooper, in their book *Mindsight*, documented 31 cases of blind people having NDEs (Ring & Cooper 1999). Dr Larry Dossey, former Chief of Staff of Medical City Dallas Hospital, describes the case of a woman who had been blind from birth being able to see clearly during her NDE:

> The surgery had gone smoothly until the late stages of the operation. Then something happened. As her physician was closing the incision, Sarah's heart stopped beating ... When she awoke Sarah had a clear, detailed memory

> of the frantic conversation of the surgeons and nurses during the cardiac arrest; the [operating room] layout; the scribbles on the surgery schedule board in the hall outside; the color of the sheets covering the operating table; the hairstyle of the head scrub nurse; the names of the surgeons in the doctors' lounge down the corridor who were waiting for her case to be concluded; and even the trivial fact that her anesthesiologist that day was wearing unmatched socks. All this she knew even though she had been fully anesthetized and unconscious during the surgery and the cardiac arrest. But what made Sarah's vision even more momentous was the fact that, since birth, she had been blind.
> (Dossey 1989)

It is not unusual for people who experience a death experience to have instantly developed what might be called psychic abilities. Dr Raymond Moody studied hundreds of people who had death experiences and found that after their death experience, they had up to four times more verifiable psychic experiences than the average population (Moody 1975). An article by the International Association of Near Death Studies (IANDS) states that "there's no denying that experiencers become quite intuitive afterward. Psychic displays can be commonplace, such as out-of-body episodes, manifestation of 'beings' met in near-death state, 'remembering' the future, finishing another's sentence, 'hearing' plants and animals 'speak'" (Atwater 2021).

After his NDE, Dannion Brinkley has used his new psychic abilities to help others. He was able to help solve the 1993 murder of John and Nancy Bosco of Bigfork, Montana, USA, who were shot to death execution style as they slept. Brinkley gave the police an accurate description of the killer, who was subsequently identified as Shadow Clark. To verify Dannion's psychic powers, Dr William Roll observed him in a series of tests.

Dannion gave readings for eight people whom he had never met before, picking out certain details about these individuals that he would not have known. Dr Roll was convinced that he was legitimate.

Some people's beliefs around death change dramatically when they have a death experience. Dr George Ritchie was convinced of two things after his death experience. First, "that our consciousness does not cease with physical death; that it becomes in fact keener and more aware than ever." And second, "that how we spend our time on Earth, the kind of relationships we build, is vastly, infinitely more important than we can know" (Ritchie 1978).

The accounts of death experiences inform you of some of what awaits you at your death. While these death experiences were involuntary, some individuals have deliberately and consciously explored the death experience to bring you more information on what lies in store for you after death.

Chapter 13

Shared Death Wisdom

There are many similarities between the accounts of death experiences and descriptions in sacred literature, such as that found in the *Tibetan Book of the Dead*. These ancient texts were the result of many years of observation and practice by advanced practitioners and should not be dismissed as fantasies of more primitive societies. While the descriptions contained in these ancient scriptures may be of their time and culture, many aspects are relevant to what we encounter today after the death of the physical body. They can still serve as practical guides for helping us and assisting others through those experiences.

The *Tibetan Book of the Dead,* or the Bardo Thodol, charts the Tibetan Buddhist stages of death and after death. It is also known as "The Great Liberation upon Hearing in the Intermediate State." Padma Sambhava wrote it in the eighth century AD and hid it for a later era. Karpa Lingpa discovered it in the fourteenth century. The *Tibetan Book of the Dead* is a guided meditation traditionally read by a lama at the bedside of someone who is dying to help them through the various intermediate "bardo" states between death and rebirth, and teach them how to attain liberation.

The source of the bardo teachings, according to Sogyal Rinpoche, author of the *Tibetan Book of Living and Dying,* is the enlightened mind, or the completely awakened mind, "as experienced, explained, and transmitted by a long line of masters that stretches back to the Primordial Buddha" (Rinpoche 1992). These masters' exploration and formulation of their discoveries over many centuries have resulted in the Tibetan Buddhist detailed picture of both life and death.

Bardo in Tibetan means "in between" or "in transition." There are four or six bardos that cover the full cycles of life, death, and rebirth. Of the six bardos, three of them occur while we are still alive: the bardo of this life covers the entire period from our birth to our death; the bardo of meditation refers to the meditative state when we are able to recognize our Buddha-nature; and the bardo of dreaming occurs while we are sleeping and can also be used to train the mind.

The other three bardo states cover the time between death and rebirth, and are the bardos of dying and death, after death, and rebirth. The bardo of dying refers to the process of dying itself. In Tibet, dying is seen as a process of purification, for we are returning to the clear light, to our intrinsic natural state of ground luminosity, dissolving in it. At the moment of death, this clear light of reality dawns for everyone. This is your own radiant nature, sometimes known as Rigpa, or enlightened wakefulness. One of the key teachings of the Bardo Thodol is that at the moment of death, you should go to the clear light of the void, go beyond all the astral realms, and merge with your spiritual essence.

However, to take advantage of this "moment of truth" so as to gain liberation, you must be prepared. Otherwise, this moment will pass by too swiftly. Because most of us are still so connected to the habits and behavior patterns we have established in life, we do not recognize ground luminosity for what it is. We react inappropriately and unconsciously. Instead of making a leap of faith and surrendering to this luminosity, we hold back. Thus, the moment passes. Buddhist lama and teacher Kalu Rinpoche's instructions for that moment of ground luminosity were to let go of body and mind, and dissolve in the clear light and be liberated in that very instant. Go beyond the snares of dualism, of life and death.

Sogyal Rinpoche says that what happens at the moment of death is that "the ordinary mind and its delusions die, and in that gap the boundless sky-like nature of our mind is uncovered. However, if we are not prepared for this, then we can miss it" (Rinpoche 1992).

If you miss the moment of liberation, you enter the second bardo state of death, where you have another opportunity to gain liberation. In this second bardo state of death, everything is a creation of your own mind and can be changed. Liberation occurs in this bardo if you can let go and surrender to the luminosity of the natural mind. If not, then you enter the third bardo of becoming, where your perceptions are returning, where you have likes and dislikes, and places and people are familiar. Your thoughts and attachments begin to assert themselves, and you are moving closer to rebirth.

According to Sogyal Rinpoche, if you do not want to miss the moment of luminosity, it is important to develop an awareness of death and to become familiar with ways to cope with the dissolution of the mind through visualization. He states that "instead of being afraid of death we may feel a sense of excitement about it" (Rinpoche 1992).

While there is a huge volume of teachings on death that can be studied in Tibetan Buddhist teachings, key aspects are that the way you have lived your life and your state of mind at the moment of death have a strong impact on your death and what happens afterwards. Much Buddhist practice is intended to see beyond the illusory experiences while alive and beyond the domains experienced after death.

Shared Death Experiences

"Shared death experiences" are occurrences that usually happen to a person or people who are at the deathbed when the person in the bed is close to dying or has just died. As the person in bed passes away, one or more of those present have experiences that appear identical to that of the dying person. These experiences are similar to those who have had a death experience. For example, they might see something leaving the body, such as a light, or a globular, grayish, golden luminosity. As the person in the bed dies, the bystander also leaves their physical body and goes partway with their loved one. Others see light filling the room, or dead relatives coming into the room to escort the relative away. Some who have accompanied a dying person partway on their journey also witness and experience the dying person's life review.

Raymond Moody, in his 2011 book *Glimpses of Eternity,* wrote that the two things in a shared death experience that he had never heard of in a near-death experience were the room changing shape and a mystical light that filled the room. He went on to say that the most startling shared death experience was the "joint review of a loved one's life" (Moody 2011).

Moody tells the story of Dana, whose husband Jim was dying of pancreatic cancer. Dana was sitting at Jim's bedside holding his hand when they both left their bodies and "began to fly through the air." Dana recounts that they left the hospital room, swooped over the city, and heard enchanting music that rose in pitch as they climbed higher over the city. They headed for a beautiful, vibrant, and powerful bright light overhead that Dana felt comfort and joy being close to. Dana saw Jim smiling and staring directly at the light, and as she was sucked back into her body she knew that Jim had died and that she had gone partway to heaven with him.

Moody thinks that "shared death experiences could come to prove that the light and all of the good things that come from it originate outside of the dying person's brain, where others can share them." The implications of this were clear: "that death opens a portal to the 'other side'" (Moody 2011).

In his book *Seven Reasons to Believe in the Afterlife,* Jean-Jacques Charbonier shares the experience of Dr Jean-Pierre Postel, an anesthetist present at his father's final moments in a resuscitation cubicle, who found himself in the tunnel of light along with his wife, who is also a doctor, and his son, who is a nurse. During the time that the three of them were at the dying man's side, they all saw the same scene: a mist separating out from the dying man's thorax. They also had the privilege of being present at the touching departure of this entity through the tunnel of light (Charbonier 2012).

Colm Keane writes about a shared death experience told to him by Martha from Cork, Ireland. Sitting at her father's bedside about two days before he died, she suddenly felt as if she was in a vastness extending to infinity that was welcoming and comforting, and heard a message saying, "This is reality." Then, she was in an illuminated cave or tunnel with her father on her left, and in front of her father was a kind of doorway or opening, beside which was a screen with pictures. Although she didn't see the content, she knew that her father was having a life review. She heard, "It's yourself you have to face." Her father had a blissful look and an aura of "glowing happiness" around him. She heard further messages: "He knows" and "Everyone should be like this," and then she found herself back in her body in the hospital. The experience changed Martha and her outlook on life, giving her a new perspective on death as being the biggest moment of our lives (Keane 2010).

Two questions most commonly asked in the life reviews of those who experienced death experiences are "What have you accomplished in your life?" and "What have you learned in the way of love and wisdom?" The message that most bring back with them is to love more. Betty Eadie, who herself had a death experience, wrote that she was "struck again and again that those who have entered into God's light at the end of life return with a simple and beautiful message: 'Love is Supreme'" (Eadie 1992).

Chapter 14

Here Comes Nothing

You are Nothing – and Everything. If you believe that there is nothing after your body dies, then that is what you will most likely experience. Accounts from Michael Newton's "life between life" sessions indicate that you will stay in this state until you reach the point where you start looking for something else; then your guides will come and assist you (Newton 1994).

If you have strongly held views on a certain type of hereafter, then that is what you will gravitate towards, and you may miss out initially on an even more rewarding and enlightening experience. So, while there are different accounts of the hereafter in this book, it helps to keep an open mind on the exact experience you will have when you leave your dead body. If you believe that there is nothing after the death of the body, it is not my intention to try to convince you otherwise. All I ask is that you look into the evidence from the many sources mentioned in this book and make up your own mind.

The concept of "nothing" is intriguing and raises questions as to what it is like to experience it, and even how nothing can exist. What is nothing? To describe or even understand nothing, there must be something present. If nothingness needs the presence of something to exist, then it is itself something. I am not aware of the existence or experience of "nothing" in this life. If it is not present in the here and now, then how or why would it exist in the hereafter, and what are the properties of nothingness? "Nothing," I hear you say. No light, no sound, no thought, no smell – nothing. Strangely, the thought of that seems attractive. It must be very peaceful, and if it is peaceful, then it is something. Of course, if it is not peaceful, then it is also something.

There is no evidence of nothingness after death. There is less proof of nothingness than there is of something. For those who are skeptical of death experiences and communication from the hereafter, a viable alternative to the hereafter has not been proven. Even if the increasingly frequent espousal of a state of nothingness after death were true, it would probably be the only occurrence of nothingness in the whole universe. Buddhist scholar Robert Thurman says that "Tibetans have the commonsense view that life is boundless, that we did not come out of nothing and cannot become nothing. We are both beginningless and endless" (Thurman 1994). Just as something cannot come out of nothing, the something that you are cannot become nothing.

Occam's razor is a philosophical principle that gives precedence to simplicity, stating that, when faced with the choice of two competing hypotheses, the simpler explanation is to be preferred. When applied to the concept of nothingness after this life, the assumptions of nothingness are more complex and more lacking in evidence than the existence of something, as evidenced by death experiences and communications from the hereafter.

The process of death has been described as a gradual dissolution of our senses and physical powers. Christine Longaker, who is a pioneer in hospice care and an expert in end-of-life care, describes the process:

> [The] external aspect of this dissolution concludes when we exhale our last breath. Yet after this point, an internal process of dissolution still continues, during which our internal energies collapse along with the thought-states of anger, desire, and ignorance which had supported our ego. The conclusion of this inner dissolution is the final moment of death, which most of us will experience as "fainting" into a dark void — a space which is peaceful and free of pain.
> (Longaker 1997)

A similar description is found in Tao Malachi's book *Gnosis of the Cosmic Christ*. He writes that "essentially, death and dying is the process of the dissolution of the gross and subtle elements of consciousness into the primordial nature of consciousness ... thus, dying and death is the return of the soul to God and the Godhead" (Malachi 2005).

Tao Malachi goes on to give a detailed description of the dying process that may appear complicated, involving the dissolution of one element into another until the final dissolution into spirit-space, which then dissolves into itself. Yet he states that "if one is aware of it and understands it, one can transform the dying process into a vehicle of self-realization and thus experience the resurrection and ascension at the time of one's death."

The *Tibetan Book of Living and Dying* details a somewhat similar process of outer and inner dissolution during the dying process (Rinpoche 1992). A broad summary involves our life-force energies dissolving and moving towards the heart center, followed by a fainting into peace and darkness, from which there is an awakening into the luminosity and vastness of your true nature, and an opening into the bardo of death. Since all conscious life has this essential nature, everyone who dies will experience this infinite luminosity. Yet what unfolds afterwards will depend on how spiritually prepared we are.

Experienced Buddhist practitioners can recognize the dawning of "ground luminosity" and unite with it effortlessly. For those who lack familiarity with the innermost nature of mind, the luminosity at death may not be recognized. According to the *Tibetan Book of Living and Dying*, "they are plunged into a state of unconsciousness, which can last up to three and a half days. It is then that the consciousness finally leaves the body" (Rinpoche 1992). The book also states that "For someone who has prepared and practiced, death comes not as a defeat but as a triumph, the crowning glory and most glorious moment of life." In the foreword to the *Tibetan Book of Living and Dying*, the Dalai

Lama writes: "The actual point of death is also when the most profound and beneficial experience can come about."

While there are some similarities between the Tibetan Buddhist viewpoint and death experiences, the Tibetan Buddhist view of the hereafter differs from many death experiences and life-between-life accounts. In the *Tibetan Book of the Dead,* it is said that there is a certain amount of time in which the person remains near the body. This is not the experience of those who have had death experiences. In such accounts, after leaving the body, they lose interest in it.

Your death experience will be unique to you. How you live your life, how you inform yourself about the moments of death, and how you have prepared for your dying moments all contribute to the death experience that you will have. The concept of nothing existing after death is inherently difficult to measure or observe scientifically, so there is little or no support or training for such an eventuality. The accounts of death from many sources indicate that whatever beliefs, thinking, and perceptions you hold or are held by your culture or tradition, consciously or subconsciously at the time of death, are what you will experience.

Chapter 15

The Bumpy Bits

There are no speed bumps in a cul-de-sac. In your journey to your ultimate destination in the hereafter, you may experience a few bumpy bits. Some accounts of what happens after death, when you leave the physical body behind, mention places and encounters that you may prefer not to have. A few people who had death experiences appear to have had a disturbing or traumatic experience, often referred to as "hellish" death experiences. The actual number or percentage of those who experience hellish experiences is not clear. In his 1975 study, Raymond Moody did not encounter any (Moody 1975). However, according to research by Penny Sartori, about 15 percent of near-death experiences are said to be hellish (Sartori 2014).

In her book *Return from Death,* Margot Grey notes several aspects of Hell-like NDEs. These include feelings of fear and panic, an out-of-body experience, entering a black void, sensing an evil force, and entering a Hell-like environment (Grey 1985). According to Christine Longaker, "some published near-death experiences describe desolate landscapes, terrifying experiences of being chased or harassed, or of witnessing entire worlds filled with beings in various states of suffering" (Longaker 1997).

In the *Tibetan Book of Living and Dying,* Rinpoche writes that not all near-death experiences are positive. He goes on to say that due to one's state of mind at death, "some people report terrifying experiences of fear, panic, loneliness, desolation, and gloom, vividly reminiscent of the descriptions of the bardo of becoming" (Rinpoche 1992).

Images of biblical judgment often feature scenes where some go on to eternal bliss and others are sent to "Hell." If you believe in Hell or have a subconscious or past-life belief in Hell that you have carried in this lifetime, then you may experience some hellish experiences when you die, more so if you believe that you may be deserving of Hell.

It is interesting to note the different accounts of hellish experiences in the various books of the dead and religious traditions. The Hells in the Tibetan and Egyptian underworlds were dark, dangerous, and ominous, with many demons, ordeals, and cruel punishments, through which the deceased passed during their spiritual journey. The Christian Hell, from which it is said there is no escape, is described in terms of a land of darkness, gnashing of teeth, fire, and separation from God. On the other hand, the Irish *Tir na nOg* is one of the best-known versions of the Celtic hereafter and is depicted as a beautiful and timeless place where people never age or die. Some mortals and heroes could visit and return from *Tir na nOg*, and it is far from a place of suffering.

George Ritchie talks about the hellish realm he was shown in his death experience. It was "a place where people no longer belonged to Earth but could not escape it either — couldn't escape the involvements, the hungers, the pride they had allowed to dominate them there" (Ritchie 1978).

The majority of hellish death experiences include visions of fire or sensations of being surrounded by flames. Yet, when help is called for, the hellish experience dissipates. Neurosurgeon Eben Alexander experienced a place where he felt stuck for a time, but from which he emerged with the assistance of what he called "the beautiful girl on the butterfly wing" (Alexander 2012).

Betty Eadie talks about moving through a black mass before entering the tunnel of light, and although she said common sense told her that she should have been terrified, she felt a profound sense of well-being and calmness within this black mass. She was aware of other people, and animals. She also sensed that "there were some who were not moving forward as I but were lingering in this wonderful blackness. They either didn't have the desire, or simply didn't know how to proceed. But there was no fear" (Eadie 1992).

In the accounts of the outer or lower levels of darkness and little light, some people appear stuck there. These are individuals who have not yet been able to rise above their deeds or thoughts during their earthly lives. Those who now reside in these dark zones of the hereafter through their intention will remain there until they are ready to be brought out of it; until their guides can enter their energy and place new thoughts and suggestions there. Nothing is keeping them there except themselves, and beings of light are ready and waiting to assist them when they are ready.

Dr Brian Weiss, psychiatrist, hypnotherapist, and author of the book *Many Lives, Many Masters*, describes the case of one of his patients, a Catholic attorney, who under hypnosis had a hellish experience amid fires and devils after a past-life death. Weiss was surprised by this extremely rare occurrence and waited for his patient to say what was happening. The client finally identified a spiritual figure as Jesus, who said to him, "Don't you realize that this is all illusion – only love is real," upon which "the fires and devils instantly disappeared revealing the beautiful light that had been there, unseen behind the illusion" (Weiss 2000).

Weiss goes on to say that:

> Intellect is important in the three-dimensional world, but intuition is more important. You have reversed reality and illusion. Reality is the recognition of your immortality, divinity, and timelessness. Illusion is your transient three-dimensional world. This reversal is damaging to you. You yearn for the illusion of security instead of the security of wisdom and love. You yearn to be accepted when, in reality, you can never be rejected. Ego creates

illusion and hides truth. Ego must be dissolved, then truth can be seen.

In the thousands of life-between-life cases that Michael Newton has conducted, and many thousands more conducted by facilitators from the Newton Institute, there has been no evidence found of the existence of a purgatory or hell in the hereafter. According to Newton, "These are outdated human conceptions designed to frighten susceptible people into religious interpretations of proper conduct in life" (Newton 2009).

There is a wonderful example in Newton's book about a client in a life-between-life session who recounted seeing a "devil" when he passed. In the particular lifetime when he died, he had been a preacher in one of the southern states in the USA and had preached fire and brimstone. The devil-type figure that he saw when he died was his spiritual guide wearing a devil mask to play a trick on him.

Newton is quite clear that "For thousands of years, religious dogma and superstition around the world has predicted we are due for punishment and retribution for our sins at the time of death. This is all false. The Spirit World is a space of love and forgiveness" (Newton 2009).

When consciousness floats free of the body, it enters a thought-responsive environment. It is so open that any thoughts or feelings one has immediately become a reality. So, whatever beliefs you hold in this lifetime at the time of your death can immediately manifest in the hereafter, if and when your thoughts turn to them. This is true of heavenly and hellish experiences.

There are lower levels in the hereafter where some people go due to their beliefs, or lack of them, at the time of death, and also because of how they have lived their lives. If you hold the awareness of these levels in your consciousness, then you may experience them. However, if your thoughts are predominantly of a higher existence, then your main experience will be of that.

During your transition, hold the thought and feeling of love as much as you can. Whatever images appear for you, bring your focus to one of love. If something fearful arises, send it love. Holding the space of love creates greater space for love. Holding the feeling of love enhances the energy of love around you. You attract what you resonate with, so the more love you can think and feel, the more love and loving experiences you will have.

Chapter 16

Good Grief

Grief — you gotta love it too. You gotta acknowledge the presence of grief, and you gotta allow it to come when it comes and allow it to leave when it leaves. Grief is most commonly experienced at the death of a loved one. It can also be felt at the passing of a pet, at the end of a meaningful relationship, or at some other happening where you are feeling deep loss. If you prize some possession dearly and it is lost or stolen from you, you can experience grief. Examining the many aspects of grief gives you insights into how you respond to the ending of something significant in your life. It also sheds light on where you may need to focus to begin shifting your awareness to one of loving death.

Grief is one of the strongest emotions you can experience. Grief can come in waves. The first waves can sometimes seem like a tsunami that sweeps you away in a flood of emotions and unexpected feelings that can be physical and emotional. The physical manifestations of grief can be unexpected and feel overpowering. They can take the form of a gut-wrenching feeling that can be painful, a sensation of tightness in the chest and throat area, being oversensitive to outside noise, weakness, lethargy, and breathlessness.

Somewhere in between the physical and emotional pains are the sensations of numbness and emptiness commonly felt after the death of a loved one. Emotions such as sadness, fear, anger, resentment, confusion, shame, love, depression, numbness, shock, joy, guilt, and more can come over you, leaving you wondering what the heck is happening to you.

Grief can be overwhelming and can affect your daily life and how you function. The overriding feelings might be "I wish that this feeling would go away" or "I don't want to feel like this." Yet the way to transcend this experience is to go into it and through it. Otherwise, little will change, as what you resist persists.

So, feel the grief that you are experiencing in all its aspects. There are advantages to the pains of grief that you are feeling. In his book *A New Earth: Awakening to Your Life's Purpose*, Eckhart Tolle writes that "The fire of suffering becomes the light of consciousness" (Tolle 2005). Make your grief conscious. Be aware of it. Choose the grief, choose the suffering, and allow the transformation to happen. Things have changed in you and in your relationship with your loved one who has passed. What you are experiencing are the feelings of change.

Grief is a calling to experience life fully without suppressing your feelings or emotions. Grief needs your attention. The physical, mental, and emotional symptoms are your indicators for processing your grief. Give yourself permission to grieve. Acknowledge and face your feelings openly and honestly; express them to yourself and others; and allow them to be, as you process all the symptoms for as long as it takes. The more you allow your feelings to be, the more quickly they will flow through you and from you.

Grief can affect us all in different ways. While grief involves immersion in your thoughts, it is also a time to be kind to yourself. Looking after yourself both physically and emotionally at times of grief helps you work through it. Consider pampering your physical body by going for a massage or some other physical treatment where you give yourself time to relax and just be. Help is always available, either through friends and family or through professional support in the form of counseling and other therapies. Sometimes, just sitting down with a good friend and talking about the person who has passed is helpful. Talking about the good times and also acknowledging and talking about the not-so-happy memories all help to deal with the emotions that you are feeling after the death of someone close.

It is not possible to put a time limit on grief, as the amount and intensity of grief vary considerably. At some stage, your grief will fade away. This does not mean forgetting about the person. Rather, it involves completely letting go. Letting go is not a betrayal of your loved one; it is liberating them, and you.

Grief is rarely considered to be a positive experience. Yet every experience can be positive if you see it as such. On a human level, your grief is enabling you to appreciate the loss of a loved one. It also gets you more in touch with yourself. Grief is more about you than the person who has died.

The theme of this book is that death is not an ending, that death is not a loss; it is a shift in your relationship with your loved ones and with yourself. This runs contrary to the current collective thinking around death. So, when someone you love dies, you are not only experiencing your loss but are also picking up on the loss that is present in the collective consciousness of humanity, including its deepest feelings of despair and longing. Mourners and family members freely express their feelings to you, reinforcing how "terrible" and "sad" it all is. Shifting from this thinking and way of being can take a conscious effort on your part.

Separating yourself from the collective consciousness on everyday issues is not necessarily easy. It can be even more difficult in the grieving process of the death of a loved one. Yet this is a call to do just that; to be part of shifting the energy around death and grief to a new and different level of awareness.

Amid your deep feelings and profound experiences, the light of knowing can slowly or suddenly emerge, revealing the perfection of all of existence. It seems contradictory, but beneath the pain and grief of loss, there is an endless well of joy and love that is ever present yet mostly untapped.

Every perceived "loss" is a prompt to focus more and more on the spiritual aspects of our existence, and not just to see everything as solely about this physical lifetime. Every loss creates a space that opens up in front of you, inviting you to fill it with something new.

We are not taught or trained in how to shift our relationship into one that is energetic rather than physical. Some people do this automatically, and others do not do it at all. While there are many ways to shift your awareness, some of the old ways are often the best. Walking in nature, meditation, body movement such as yoga, tai chi, or labyrinth walking, all help to clear the mind and support the body in letting go of the energy of loss that it may be holding on to.

You have more control over the emotions of grief than you might think. Emotions are your guidance system in this world. The more you become aware of your emotions, the more you recognize what is happening with you. This does not mean that when you become aware of whatever emotion you are in, it is somehow easier. It means that you now have the key to exploring what is happening and an opportunity to learn about yourself.

Emotions are a vibration, and as you can change your vibration, you can therefore change your emotions. The first step in this is to identify the emotion that you are experiencing. Putting a label on the emotion shifts your perspective from being in your emotion to your emotion being in you. Separating the emotion from who you are further breaks the hold that an emotion has on you. You are not your emotions; you are experiencing an emotion. When you see an emotion as separate from who you are, you can then begin to consider what has brought about the emotion and move on to whether or not you wish to have that emotion remain in you.

When identifying a current emotion, do not give it ownership of you. Using the words "I am" followed by naming the emotion directly associates it with your energy and makes it more difficult to separate you from the emotion that you are experiencing. Instead, identify the emotion with statements such as "There is an emotion in me," "There is grief in me," or "I am experiencing grief at the moment." The Irish language has a wonderful way of expressing emotions in that having emotions is translated as the emotion being "on" you. For example, *Ta bron orm* translates literally as "There is sadness on me," or *Ta athas orm* as "There is happiness on me."

The emotions of death tend to put the focus on ourselves. The more we become consumed by the emotions that we are experiencing, the longer they will last, and the more difficult it will be to shift ourselves from them. When we shift our awareness away from ourselves to the one who has passed, our emotions and their intensity change.

Your thinking and beliefs about death deeply impact the level of emotion that you feel at the death of a loved one. Just as emotions are your teacher, Death is your professor — your ultimate teacher. When you see death as a transition and can connect with the energy and presence of your loved one, it becomes easier to live with the perceived loss.

Grief is primarily about you, not the recently deceased. Grief is about your sense of loss. When much of your identity is embedded in the physical presence of the person who has died, you will feel the loss more. When part of you is invested in the other person, you will feel the loss of that part of you at their death. The more you consider you have lost when someone dies, the more loss and its associated suffering you will experience.

"What we mourn is ourselves." So wrote Stephen Levine, who went on to say, "Know that it is you who you are mourning and make room in your heart for yourself. It is the pain in your heart that you feel, not the pain of another" (Levine 1982). Know also that there is a meaning for everything, including grief. Yet there is very little training available in advance to empower you to be prepared for how grief may affect you and how you might see and work with grief differently. The available training is aimed mostly at professionals and healthcare workers.

When grief arises, you are mainly left to rely on whatever ways you have already learned of dealing with loss. Just as with death, grief is mostly considered to be negative. The positive aspects of grief, such as contributing to personal growth, emotional healing, and transformation, are rarely considered. When you recognize and embrace these positive aspects of grief, you begin to shift to a place of loving grief. You will start to see that grief has a wonderful place in life and death. Grief — you gotta love it too.

Chapter 17

Attached to Grief

Grief is related to attachment. If you are not attached to something, you most likely do not feel grief. The more you live in attachment, the more grief you will experience. Christine Longaker encapsulated this concept when she wrote that "The depth of pain we experience in grief is connected to our degree of attachment to the person and how much he or she was integral to our sense of well-being" (Longaker 1997). In his book *Who Dies?*, Stephen Levine writes:

> Whatever you want, the more you want it, the more there is a kind of grief, a sickness, a hollowness in the pit of the stomach. Whether it is the desire to see a loved one again, or to stay alive, or to die, or to be successful, or for some new shiny bauble, the very nature of such longing has a quality of grief about it.
> (Levine 1982)

When you are engulfed by grief and its deep emotions, you are still relating primarily to the physical form of the person who has passed. Death changes the relationship you have with the person who has died. You were attached to the old form of the person you loved and were accustomed to being in their physical presence. Yet everything is changing; the person you love has changed. Seeing them as they are now, not as the physical characteristics that they had when in a body, is essential to establish that new form of relationship. Shifting from that old perspective into a now nonphysical one takes a conscious effort. Your grief is primarily attached to the past, and your grieving is the process of you changing.

Just as your loved one has changed and become something else, so you must seek the understanding of this change. You are also becoming something else in every moment. Allow your awareness of the changes that are happening to you to be in the present. Rather than being absorbed with how things were, start seeing and feeling how things are now.

Writing about her journey after her son Bryan was killed in a senseless act of murder, Paige Lee said that one of the most important understandings she gained was that she "needed to be open to receiving Bryan as he is now, not as the sandy-haired boy that I had birthed and nurtured for twenty-three years, because his physical presence was indeed gone" (Lee 2020). Lee went on to add that "Nothing has really changed, except that their physical bodies are gone."

Your loved one has not become nothing. They exist in a different dimension. You need to use different senses to know and "see" them in their current existence. The greater your resistance to this change, the deeper your experience of grief will be. Robert Schwartz, author of the book *Your Soul's Plan*, summarized grief, attachment, and change in the context of impermanence: "When you understand impermanence, when you understand that change is the only constant in a space-time continuum, then you understand that such losses come and go" (Schwartz 2007).

There is a difference between attachment and love. The adage "If you love them, set them free" applies equally and as strongly in death as in life. Love is your natural state of being that you share unconditionally with your loved ones. It includes happiness in seeing your loved ones experience the joys of life. Attachment is conditional on something being present in the form you wish it to be. You can move from attachment to love by seeing your loved ones embracing the joys of death and the hereafter. Your grief and the death of a loved one are calling you to simultaneously experience your human sorrow and your divine love and joy. The key is finding a balance between experiencing your grief and allowing the deceased person to go.

Amid this mingling joy and pain, you are also being given the experience of seeing yourself and your life in a new light. Frank Ostaseski, co-founder of the Zen Hospice Project, writes:

> Grief … opens us to the most essential truths of our lives: the inevitability of impermanence, the causes of suffering, and the illusion of separateness. We begin to appreciate that we are more than the grief. We are what the grief is moving through.
> (Ostaseski 2017)

Communication beyond Grief

One of the disadvantages of grief is that it prevents your deceased loved one from communicating easily with you. Accounts from those who have died support the view that grief is a significant barrier to their making meaningful contact with you. When you are engrossed in the feelings and emotions of grief, these feelings are often all-consuming; nothing else gets in, not even your loved ones who have transitioned.

What we mostly do not recognize is that grief can have a negative effect on our loved ones who have passed, who are seeking to make contact with us. In the book *The Bridge over the River*, a soldier named Sigwart, who died during the First World War, was able to communicate with his sisters. He said to them, "Your grief tormented me at the beginning for I had made the greatest effort to make myself susceptible to you. It is better now" (Sigwart 1972).

Erik Medhus was also deeply aware of and affected by the grief of his family. Erik Medhus was just 20 years old when he took his own life and entered the hereafter. His mother, Elisa, had been raised by two atheists and had become a physician.

She was a complete skeptic when it came to the idea of life after death. Several events happened through Erik trying to make contact, and Elisa decided to have a channeling session with spirit translator James Butler. Erik and Elisa realized that they had a soul contract to support those experiencing pain and grief. Elisa set up a blog called "Channeling Erik," and Erik began taking part. Together, they would blog, write books, and make videos to help people live happier, more loving lives and to have faith in the great return to love that awaits us after death (Medhus 2015).

In his book *My Life after Death*, Erik Medhus shares the entire story of his death and the events he experienced afterwards. The fear Erik sensed in his loved ones was something he wanted to help them with. He wanted to assure them that their consciousness remains after death and to enable them to see death as a transition rather than a permanent separation. This was the beginning of his role as a spirit guide to help free humanity from the fear of death.

Eric describes the sometimes-difficult process of contacting mourning relatives in quite strong language. He said:

> It's fucking hard for spirits to slow down enough to reach people who are grieving because they vibrate at the bottom of the visible part of the energy spectrum. This is why people use terms like, "I'm depressed," "I'm feeling low," or "I'm feeling down."
> (Medhus 2015)

One of Erik Medhus's guides in Heaven showed him how to send energetic cords out everywhere to create a web. The cords create a pattern that brings order that he needs the human to see and feel on a subconscious level, giving them the direction they need to take: "When people get stuck in emotions, they get tangled up in the cords because they focus on the chaos instead of the orderly pattern. Subconsciously sensing this web of order helps them recognize that things aren't as random and chaotic as they think" (Medhus 2015).

Those grieving who wish to make contact with their deceased loved ones must keep an open channel for communication. If the living are consumed by their grief and emotions, then they are not in a space to establish lines of communication. If the living no longer think of the dead, assuming that everything ends with death, then the dead cannot reach them. In an increasingly materialistic world, this is becoming more prevalent.

Psychologist Hans Stolp says that "The dead can only make contact with an element in the human soul that is spiritual and unselfish" (Stolp 2017). He goes on:

> The result is that many of the dead will not be able to contact their partners, family members, or friends. This not only results in spiritual loneliness on both sides, but also hinders the help, inspiration, and encouragement which the dead can, in their turns, give from the spiritual world.

Our grieving can truly affect loved ones in their transition to their new way of being. In the *Tibetan Book of Living and Dying,* Sogyal Rinpoche says that "if a dead person has to watch her loved ones distraught and helpless with grief, it could plunge her into deep grief also" (Rinpoche 1992).

Sigwart also described the grief that his deceased mother experienced in the hereafter, saying to his relatives:

> You have hurt her by mourning for her. One may not grieve for a departed one. We remain united exactly as on Earth, although the bereaved ones are not able to perceive it. You cannot imagine what it means to us who no longer have physical bodies when someone we

> love weeps for us. This is the most severe anguish for us to endure because we still feel exactly as we did on Earth ... We feel every thought of pain the same as we did in our earthly state because we are the ones you knew and loved. Grieving creates a chasm between you and us. Later, only love remains – the highest, holiest and most intimate bond.
> (Sigwart 1972)

Michael Newton found that "Souls do not have the same overpowering grief about physical death as those who are left behind, but many feel a duty to comfort" (Newton 1994). American lawyer, author, and psychical researcher Edward C. Randall writes of his conversation through a psychic, Emily French, with a soldier killed at Gettysburg. The soldier said that

> it was sorrow for the wife and the babies; their great grief when they learned what had happened, bound me to their condition, and we sorrowed together. I could not progress or find happiness until time had healed their sorrow. If only those in earth life knew that their sadness binds and holds us, stays our progress and development!
> (Heagerty 2015)

Another female spirit speaking through Emily French said:

> The grief of my people kept me so sad at first that I was not able to see or think of anything but earthly sorrow. That is why grief for departed friends and relatives is so wrong, and is so harmful, both to those on Earth and on those who come over. The longer grief continues and the more hopeless it is, the more those mourned for are kept attached to Earth. Instead of being able to go straight on when they come over, seeing and realizing the beauty and

wonders of their surroundings, and helping others to see them also, they are kept in a state of helpless grief, which renders them incapable of either helping themselves or others.

Moving On Is Not Forgetting

Moving on is not forgetting. It is remembering in a new and more vibrant light. Moving on in the name of love is a powerful act. Remembering the eternal love that exists between you, and learning to live in that love in the physical absence of your loved one, is a gift to you and them. It does not mean that you forget them. It is a living remembrance of the wonderful times you spent together to move forward in a space of love and the joy of living.

As you move through grief, your thoughts will come around to considering your life and what it is that you still have to experience and do, while staying connected with your departed loved one. There are things you have to do just for yourself. Only you can do what you need to do. Only you can deal with what is happening in your life. Only you can learn what you have to learn and move on to the next experience.

And you are not only doing it for yourself. Everything you do is connected to others, especially your family, but also to the wider human family. What you do, you do for all of humanity. Focusing on yourself as a spiritual being, as an integral part of one great human family with its many levels of interconnectedness, brings you to a different perspective on what is happening and what you can do. When you rise above fear, when you realize that being fearful serves neither you nor anyone else, then you are taking a giant step for yourself and an important step for humanity.

In due course, in the processing of your grief, you will begin again to think about the meaning of your life. This may initially be in the form of why you are the one to have survived or been "left behind." As you experience letting go of the physical aspects of the relationship, you begin to contemplate what that person might have wished for you to do, now that they have passed. At some point, you will need to decide that your grieving is finished and that it is time to begin creating a new life for yourself. This is not about forgetting the person you were grieving, but about honoring their ongoing existence and the relationship that you had and still have now on a different level.

In the Bhagavad Gita, an ancient Indian holy text, Krishna tells Arjuna that "death is certain for the born. Rebirth is certain for the dead. You should not grieve for what is inevitable" (Easwaran 2007, 2:27). Elsewhere in the Bhagavad Gita, it is written that "The soul is spoken of as invisible, inconceivable, and unchangeable. Knowing this, you should not grieve for the body" (Easwaran 2007, 2:25).

So, let the dying die. Do not hold on tightly to them. Do not put your grief and fear of loss and endings onto them. The dying person often knows that they are about to move on. They may not fear this as much as you think. Rather than being consumed by your feelings and thoughts, focus on your loved one who has moved on. Send them thoughts and feelings of love. Send them smiles of your happy memories. Send them thanks for all the wonderful times you spent together. Know in your heart that they are aware of what you are doing. Then listen. Most of the communications from the deceased bear this out. The dead can talk. Listen to what they say.

Chapter 18

The Talking Dead

The dead are not gone. It is common for people to experience the presence of a loved one who has died. If you feel the presence of a loved one who has passed, know their energy is close to you. If you see them in a dream or have a vision of them, then know that you are still connected with them. People who have died often remain close to their physical body for several days, during which time they often visit their loved ones to say their goodbyes, and to bring them some comfort.

Deceased people regularly try to get in contact with their loved ones on Earth. A study in 2013 found that as many as three-quarters of bereaved people have sensed the presence of a deceased loved one (Keen, Murray, & Payne 2013). The presence of a deceased person can manifest in a variety of ways, from the actual form of the deceased appearing, to signs and messages such as smells, objects in unusual places, and other signs that are clear and convincing to the bereaved person.

The physical manifestation of an apparently dead person can be both reassuring and shocking. LeeAnn had a friend named Bruno who was murdered while working as a nightclub bouncer. A few months later, while at home, LeeAnn had an experience that she describes below in her own words:

> All of a sudden, the room filled with this golden light. There was a sense of peace that was overwhelming ... Then I saw Bruno in his human form. My eyes were closed, but he was standing there, surrounded by blue colors and light. He said to me, "You keep asking for me to come back. Don't ask that — this is where I'm supposed to be." (Taylor 2021)

Not all materializations or visitations are so dramatic. Irish writer Colm Keane describes how many visitations from deceased loved ones occur in the upper left corner of the room (Keane 2009). Keane cited one example of a woman named Ethna who told how her father visited her several times over a three-month period after his death in the upper left corner of the bedroom from where she was.

When you are open to having contact with someone deceased, there are several ways of doing this. One of the most common ways of contacting a deceased person is through a medium. A medium is someone who can communicate with those who are in the hereafter. Everybody has the ability to be a medium, yet few believe that they can, or trust what they are receiving. Like any ability, if you practice more you will get better at it, although some are better than others and have made mediumship their life's work.

Connecting through Mediums

There are many accounts of the dead communicating through a medium. These communications can take different forms. The most common one is when the medium relates what they are receiving from the deceased person. Some mediums in trance allow the voice and personality of the deceased person to come through them, while there are also many accounts of psychic mediums materializing deceased people, or body parts of a deceased person, while in a trance.

The extraordinary ability of Emily S. French, who lived from 1830 to 1912, is detailed in the book *The French Revelation*. She is known as one of the greatest American independent voice mediums. French held seances in darkness, during which spirit voices manifested from thin air some distance away from her, while she was not in trance. An eminent and respected businessman and celebrated trial lawyer, Edward C. Randall, intended to expose her as a fraud, but after conducting many exacting experiments to test her powers, he became completely convinced that she was genuine.

During the seances, the spirits would carry on a conversation with Randall, or whoever else he invited to the seance. Everything was recorded in detail by a stenographer, and Randall asked many searching and important questions. Randall published his own book, *Life's Progression: Research in Metapsychics*, in 1906, which included the results of his 15 years of research. In his book, he stated that he got all his information about life, death, and the hereafter "from those that are living that life; from spirits with whom I have talked voice to voice for many years" (Randall 1906). Randall said that he published his work "in the hope that the fear of death may pass, that those who mourn may find consolation, and that all may finally understand" (Heagerty 2015). On the cover of his book, he stated: "There is no death; there are no dead."

In Randall's own words:

> Night after night, Mrs. French and I sat and talked and listened in darkness. Why in darkness? do you ask. Because in light there is motion. In order that the spirit may talk with an audible voice it must, for the moment, be clothed with material. Motion disintegrates matter. Everything that ever lived was born in the dark. In this condition, then, the whispers came more distinctly. Words were uttered, sentences formed, until in time, out of the darkness, in my own home, surrounded by conditions that I myself made, voices full and clear came, filling the room, reverberating through the whole house, metapsychic voices which any could hear as well as I myself, and which many have heard. With these voices came splendid speech, great lectures, much knowledge.

Randall went on to say that he "never ceased to be startled when a voice first speaks from the invisible world — so unusual, so marvelous, so wonderful, and yet to me, so natural" (Heagerty 2015).

Randall had more than 700 sittings with French over 22 years. He wrote: "Hundreds, yea even thousands (of spirits) have come and talked with me, and to many whom I have invited to participate in the work – thousands of different voices, different personalities, no two alike, and at times in different languages" (Hogan 2020).

Another nineteenth-century medium, Lenora Piper, was tested repeatedly by a wide range of skeptical observers. Richard Hodson, one of the leading members of the Society for Psychical Research, started out as a skeptic and was determined to expose Piper as a fraud. However, in a 300-page report that included detailed descriptions of the controls he used to prevent fraud, he had no doubt that she was speaking to people living in the life after this life (Hogan 2020).

Irish medium Eileen Garret was born in County Meath, Ireland, in 1893. In one of her seances in 1930, held at the National Laboratory of Psychical Research, and organized by its founder Harry Price and a journalist, Ian D. Coster, interesting and unexpected information came through. The purpose of the seance was to try to make contact with the famous writer Arthur Conan Doyle, who had recently died.

Instead of making contact with Arthur Conan Doyle, a spirit voice came through during the seance identifying himself as Flight Lieutenant H.C. Irwin of Airship R101. The voice informed those present that the airship he had been flying had crashed on a hillside in France two days earlier, resulting in 48 of its 54 passengers being killed. Information about the crash had not yet been released by the government. Irwin provided a significant amount of technical information that was well beyond the knowledge of Eileen Garret, and all the information provided by Irwin was confirmed by the official inquiry several months later.

In the 1850s, James J. Mapes investigated many mediums in an effort to debunk them. Born in 1806, he was a professor of chemistry and natural philosophy at the National Academy of Design in New York and later at the American Institute. His efforts led him to change his views, after which he concluded:

> The manifestations which are pertinent to the ends required are so conclusive in their character as to establish in my mind certain cardinal points.
>
> These are: First, there is a future state of existence, which is but a continuation of our present state of being ... Second, that the great aim of nature, as shown through a great variety of spiritual existences, is progression, extending beyond the limits of this mundane sphere ... Third, that spirits can and do communicate with the mortals, and in all cases evince a desire to elevate and advance those they communicate with.
> (Hogan 2020)

More recent experiments to provide evidence of communication with people who have passed include the Scole Experiments and experiments by Professor Gary Schwartz. As with any communications using mediums, skeptics will expound on the reasons why these are fake, although the Schwartz experiments used many controls to eliminate cold readings (Schwartz & Simon 2002). Your thinking before you approach any information can influence your assessment of the information. If you believe in the veracity of information received by mediums, you will veer towards accepting the findings. If you believe it is all hokum, then you veer towards finding evidence to that effect. In life, healthy skepticism is a valuable companion to your inquiries. When accompanied by an open, inquiring mind, your search will lead you to many fascinating findings.

Instrumental Transcommunication

A more modern version of voice mediumship is what is known as "Electronic Voice Phenomenon" (EVP), or "Instrumental Transcommunication" (ITC). Voices, and even images, of deceased people have been captured on recording equipment, providing further evidence that consciousness functions in a nonphysical realm.

Thomas Edison, who invented the phonograph, also tried to invent a device capable of communicating with the dead. Edison wrote:

> If our personality survives, then it is strictly logical or scientific to assume that it retains memory, intellect, other faculties, and knowledge that we acquire on this Earth. Therefore ... if we can evolve an instrument so delicate as to be affected by our personality as it survives in the next life, such an instrument, when made available, ought to record something.
> (Wagner 2019)

While Edison did not succeed in inventing such a device, as technology progressed there were increasing accounts of unexplained voices appearing on recording devices, which are now recognized by some as a genuine way of receiving messages from nonphysical sources.

Friedrich Jürgenson became known as "the Father of EVP." Jürgenson was a Swedish film producer who, in 1959, was recording bird songs. When he played back the recordings, he could discern his deceased mother's voice saying in German, "Friedrich, you are being watched. Friedel, my little Friedel, can you hear me?" He subsequently recorded hundreds of such voices and wrote two books on the subject: *Voices from the Universe* and *Radio Contact with the Dead*.

When he died in 1987, an image of Jürgenson appeared during his funeral on a TV screen watched by his friends Claude and Ellen Thorlin, who captured the image with a Polaroid camera. Several years after his death, Jürgenson and the spirit group Timestream coordinated a "cross-contact," in which Jürgenson's image was seen on a TV belonging to Adolf Homes in Rivenich, Germany.

On the same day, the Harsches, a couple in Luxembourg, found a file on their computer. It was a picture of their spirit friend Swejen Salter standing in her Spirit World lab, showing the picture of Jurgenson that her group was "simulcasting" to the TV owned by Adolf Homes. They arranged cross-contacts such as this one in part as assurance that the spirit contacts were legitimate. In 1994, Jürgenson again sent his picture to Adolf's TV. This was the first color picture ever received from the other side through equipment.

A Latvian psychologist, Dr Konstantin Raudive, heard of Jürgenson's work in the 1960s. He was skeptical at first but began his own experiments in 1967, during which he too heard the voice of his deceased mother saying, "Kostulit, this is your mother." ("Kostulit" was the boyhood name she always called him.) He went on to record thousands of EVP voices (Wagner 2019).

Brazilian Sonia Rinaldi has recorded hundreds of messages from deceased children for their parents. Sonia asks questions while the recording device is switched on, and although no other voices are heard in the room during the recording, when the recording is played back there are responses to the questions she asked. For example, in one case when no one was in the room with Sonia, Sonia asked, "Would you like to leave a message to your mother?" There is a clear child's voice answering, "Mommy, I can talk" (Seek Reality, no date).

Sonia Rinaldi had an interesting experience when she attended a seance held by materialization medium David

Thompson. To eliminate any interference from Thompson, he was seated in a wooden cabinet, bound with cords and zip ties, and gagged with tape over his mouth. During the seance, a voice from someone who was not in the room asked, "Is your name Sonia?" When Sonia replied "Yes," the voice said, "There is a man that wants to speak to you." The materialized man came forward, stood before her in the dark, and spoke, saying, "Sonia, Sonia Rinaldi." Sonia replied "Yes." The man then said, "My name is Konstantin Raudive." This was in 2014, and Konstantin had been dead since 1974. Raudive went on to tell Sonia about a problem with the electronic communication she was using and the technical information she needed to resolve it.

Sheri Perl in New York learned Sonia's methods and today, on her website, has an online training video and slide show on how to record EVP (Perl 2022). In Sheri's recordings, the answers to the questions come immediately after the question, indicating that the deceased person is actively engaging in the conversation, listening to and then answering the questions.

There are many ways in which the deceased can contact us. As your openness to connecting with a deceased loved one grows, so does the possibility of communication. Knowing that after-death experiences are more common than generally talked about can also be of comfort. In their book *Hello from Heaven*, Bill and Judy Guggenheim list the many different ways in which deceased people have contacted their still-alive loved ones. Some of these include smelling a fragrance, feeling a touch, or even seeing an animal such as a butterfly or a particular bird that has a significant meaning for the person seeing it, due to its association with the deceased person (Guggenheim & Guggenheim 1996).

On their website (www.after-death.com), the Guggenheims state that between 20 and 40 percent of Americans have had one or more after-death communication incidents. In many cases, this communication from someone who had passed provided great comfort and helped those still alive to find new meaning in their lives and heal their emotional wounds.

Sometimes, communications from the deceased are not so clearly obvious but give us food for thought. Dr Charbonier describes how his father "passed to the other side of the veil" on 4 July 2006, while taking his nap (Charbonier 2012). His father was very interested in Charbonier's research into near-death experiences but was much more skeptical than Charbonier about the existence of a life after death. Nevertheless, prior to his passing, they had made an agreement that if there is a life in the hereafter, he would let Charbonier know about it by making use of the grandfather clock that dominated the corner of the dining room. On 4 July 2006, at the precise time of his death, the hands of this grandfather clock came to a definite stop. While it might just be a simple coincidence, it is worthwhile taking account of the fact that this clock had never stopped before.

The deceased speak to us in many ways, depending both on their ability to communicate and on our ability to recognize the communications. Much of the aforementioned contact has been at the initiative of the deceased, who are choosing to get in contact. These contacts are usually to let you know that they are OK or to reassure you that they are still a presence in your life, even if they are no longer there in a physical sense.

Chapter 19

Meeting the Dead

It is possible to contact and have a conversation with a deceased loved one. There are several ways in which you can make this contact. Dr Raymond Moody developed what he calls a "psychomanteum," which works on the principle that when some people gaze into a clear optical depth, they often see visions. These visions just seem to appear. This is similar to the practice of gazing into a crystal ball, or scrying using a mirror or similar shiny surface.

Moody set up a modern-day psychomanteum, or mirror room, in his home. It was inspired by Ancient Greek practices in an actual psychomanteum, or "Oracle of the Dead," that was excavated at Ephyra in Greece in the 1950s. Fragments of a giant bronze cauldron were found, suggesting that the reflective surface could have been the liquid it contained, or the polished surface of the cauldron itself. Moody arranged a darkened room with a large mirror on one wall and a chair angled so that the person seated in the chair could not see their reflection. There was a small lamp positioned behind the chair.

Moody prepared for several hours to invoke his late maternal grandmother, looking at old photographs and recalling memories. He spent an hour gazing into the mirror with no results. However, shortly afterwards, he had an encounter with his paternal grandmother in which the apparition appeared healthy and much younger than she was when she died, and also appeared to be in mental communication with him. Moody said that his relationship with this relative was healed as a result of this encounter.

Moody called his purpose-built room a "Theatre of the Mind." His findings from the events in this room are recounted in his book *Reunions* (Moody & Perry 1993). He prepared the person who was to enter by talking about the loved one who had died. He then seated the person in a chair in the room and left them alone for an hour or more. Afterwards, he spent some time with them processing what they went through.

He collated the findings from over 300 people he interviewed about their experiences in his psychomanteum. About 50 percent held conversations, either mentally or audibly, with the person who appeared to them, while roughly 25 percent encountered a deceased relative other than the one they had set out to meet. In about a quarter of cases, the apparition was encountered after the psychomanteum session, usually within 24 hours.

Moody noted that the experience of people often began with the appearance of a mist or smoke, often accompanied by lights, colors, and geometric shapes. The deceased person usually appeared healthy and younger than when they had died. Most of the people interviewed were sure that their experiences were real events, and not fantasies or dreams, and they were certain that they were in the presence of their loved ones. As in the case of death experiences, the people were powerfully affected by their encounters, with many reevaluating their views of reality and life's meaning.

Another method of contacting deceased loved ones is the process called "Induced After-Death Communication," or IADC. This was developed by clinical psychologist Allan Botkin in 1995 as a therapy for grief and loss. It uses a form of eye-movement desensitization and reprocessing, or EMDR, to enter a state of mind where the person becomes receptive to receiving after-death communication. Botkin has trained hundreds in how to administer this therapy.

In a typical IADC session, the person affected by the death of another is asked to focus directly on their sadness while following instructions to make specific eye movements.

According to Craig Hogan, writing in *Your Eternal Self: Science Discovers the Afterlife*:

> The IADCs occur when the psychotherapist helps the patient set aside anger, guilt, shame, and other negative emotions using the powerful eye movement desensitization and reprocessing therapy method. That leaves only the deep, underlying sadness. The psychotherapist then takes the person into that sadness, plumbing its depths without flinching from it, until the person has experienced the most painful reaches of it. The person, most often in tears, then closes his or her eyes and remains open to whatever will happen.
> (Hogan 2020)

Typically, the patient sees the deceased person, and the deceased person tells them that everything is OK and not to grieve. Induced After-Death Communication is said to heal the deep sadness that is associated with the death of a loved one. Most people believe that their experience is real, although belief is not necessary to benefit from it.

"Repair and Reattachment Grief Therapy" is a form of psychotherapy developed by Rochelle Wright, a Washington State licensed psychotherapist, which helps the person whose loved one is now in the hereafter to have their own connection with the deceased. In her book *Guided Afterlife Connections: They Come to Change Lives*, co-written with Craig Hogan, Wright describes how, during a session, a person whose loved one is now living in the hereafter is helped to have his or her own connection with that individual. There is no medium involved, and the messages are said to come directly to the person sitting with their eyes closed (Wright & Hogan, 2011).

Loving Heart Connections® is a modality developed by Jane Bissler that also uses eye movement desensitization and reprocessing combined with bilateral stimulation through tapping, sounds, and eye movements. It is designed to activate a spiritual connection between you and your deceased loved ones, guides, higher self, and your true nature. It involves one session, after which you will have all the information you need to continue on your own.

The Afterlife Research and Education Institute, Inc. (AREI) has goals "to encourage the development and enhancement of methods of afterlife communication, so every person is able to communicate with loved ones in the hereafter" and "to teach people how to use the methods of afterlife communication to connect with loved ones living on the other side of life." There is a free training program in the "Self-Guided Afterlife Connections" procedure available through the Afterlife Institute website with a view to "helping people relieve their grief by connecting with loved ones we know without a doubt are available and anxious to communicate" (Afterlife Research and Education Institute, Inc., no date).

This area of direct communication with deceased loved ones, while apparently practiced thousands of years ago, is being newly redeveloped with modern techniques and practices. It is not yet widely known or accepted, although the results appear to speak for themselves. It may or may not be for you. However, knowing that a means of communication exists can be a great comfort, even if you never use it.

Chapter 20

Life in the Hereafter

When you leave the physical body, your life continues in a new way. We can compile a fairly comprehensive picture of what awaits you when you die by putting together the accounts of those who have experienced death, those who have traveled deeper into consciousness, those who remember being in the hereafter while in hypnosis or otherwise, and the accounts of deceased people communicating with their loved ones and through mediums. Life in the hereafter will be different for everyone, just as life here on Earth is different. Yet some common themes and experiences can shed light on what you might expect.

In addition to what all others have experienced and related for our benefit, you also bring your unique presence to your existence in the hereafter. In a nutshell, what you believe you will experience is what you experience. If you believe that there is nothing after death, then you will experience nothing. If you believe that you will meet Jesus, or Buddha, or some other spiritual master, then you will meet them. If you believe that you will meet a deceased loved one, then you will. If you have no beliefs or expectations, then you need to be aware of your every thought. The experiences you have all stem from your thoughts creating your reality. As the hereafter is a thought-responsive environment, what you think is what you immediately experience. In many aspects, life in the hereafter is also an illusion, just like Earth, where everything is a joint creation of ourselves and others.

The starting point for an exploration of the hereafter is this current physical realm, in which we can physically touch, feel, and sense what is around us. It is what we commonly consider to be reality, although many spiritual teachers say that this "reality" is an illusion — the *maya* of Hindu teachings. When we scratch the surface of this so-called physical reality, we uncover a mystical world of nonphysical experiences. Jurgen Ziewe, who spent many hundreds of hours in full waking consciousness outside of his body, discovered through his out-of-body travels that "the dimensions surrounding us are not spatially separated at all but interpenetrate each other in the same way as we can observe different wavelengths in the same space" (Ziewe 2008). This can help explain the ease which some people have in contacting their deceased loved ones, and also how we contact them in dreams and other nonphysical experiences.

An out-of-body experience (OBE) is where part of your consciousness remains in the physical body while a significant portion of your consciousness is active within the nonphysical environment. Some observers consider that a phrase such as "accessing the greater consciousness" is a more accurate term for what happens, as it puts the focus on consciousness rather than the body.

During an out-of-body experience, a connection is always maintained between the part of you that is having an out-of-body experience and your physical body. This is the "silver cord" referred to in many accounts and traditions. There is nothing unusual about out-of-body experiences. They are natural occurrences that happen to most of us every night when we are asleep. When we sleep, we enter the spiritual realms of reality. Some out-of-body experiences can occur because of a traumatic incident and can be very similar to death experiences.

When you leave the current physical realm at death, you experience life and consciousness in a completely different way. There is relief from any physical pain, and you become aware of the absence of any weight or mass that might be linked to identity. You have 360-degree vision and a hearing ability that can be described as an inner hearing. You will experience the hereafter as more real than the physical environment that you left on Earth. Depending on the level of the hereafter at which you meet others, you most likely will mentally project a virtual body similar to your most recent earthly one, but in the prime of your life. As you progress, you learn to master the skills needed to function fully in the nonphysical world, primarily through focused intention.

Robert Monroe was a pioneer of out-of-body experiences. He founded the Monroe Institute, which recorded much information about human consciousness and its various states, including details of the hereafter that he and others explored. Other well-known out-of-body travelers who have recounted details of the hereafter include William Buhlman and Jurgen Ziewe. They all found that there is a vast array of places that your consciousness can go to in the hereafter. Where you go and what you experience depends on you, your thoughts and beliefs, and your level of awareness. The accounts of the hereafter reflect what Yeshua (Jesus) said in the Bible, in John chapter 14, verse 2: "In my Father's house there are many mansions."

There is a halfway stage between this life and the hereafter in which the consciousness of those who are in a coma or under the intoxicating effects of certain types of drugs resides. Beyond this stage, there are the levels and realms experienced by those who have died.

The first level is inhabited by those who have passed and become stuck after leaving their physical body, and who may be quite confused. They often do not realize that they have died, and their consciousness is focused on the physical world. Some cannot understand why those in physical life seem to be ignoring them. There are always spiritual helpers available for everyone, but help for those stuck in this level comes more easily from those residing in the physical world, who can guide them to the help available in the spiritual realm.

Those who do not have any belief in the hereafter may find themselves stuck in a state of apparent nothingness created by their thoughts. Matthew McKay shared information from his deceased son Jordan, writing that people's energy form will stay in these bardo states

> until guides can enter their energy patterns and drop in new suggested images and thoughts. It is like trying to wake someone from a deep sleep — nudging and pushing and whispering, and finally shouting and rocking them. The guides are required to make more and more forceful interventions until these confused souls begin awakening to their life in spirit.
> (McKay 2021)

Jordan goes on to advise that the first and foremost task of an arriving soul is "listening for love." You first meet a vibration of love, and it may come to you in several ways, depending on how you best communicate. You may hear the sound of love, feel the warmth of love, or see the vibrant light of love. So, as far as you can, empty your mind of thoughts and "listen, see, and feel for love in all directions."

Ziewe considers that for the average person, dying will be no more traumatic than going to sleep, because very little will have changed when arriving on the other side (Ziewe 2008). He goes on to say that "many will take some convincing that they are dead, as the first impression is that they feel just as alive as before. Nature's laws of attraction gradually kick in and connect us to our natural energy environment." This could be the proverbial Heaven or Hell, as death is not an automatic ticket to the proverbial Heaven.

Moving further into the spiritual world are the belief realms, called the "Belief System Territories" by the Monroe Institute. Here we find the Heavens of all major religions inhabited by groups of people who are attracted to each other by their shared religious beliefs. These are collective thought-realities created by commonly held beliefs, and by centuries and more of teachings on Earth. A person will reside here for as long as they share the beliefs of the group. But at some point, a person may begin to question or notice inconsistencies in that particular doctrine. When they no longer resonate with that particular group, they move on to another level of awareness in the hereafter.

William Buhlman refers to these realms as "consensus realities," saying that they are stable energy constructs created by the collective power of many minds. He says that "this kind of energy environment is highly resistant to change." Buhlman writes elsewhere that during the 40 years of his out-of-body explorations, he made the startling observation that "a large percentage of individuals after death remain cloistered within nonphysical realities (heavens) that exist close in vibration to the physical world" (Buhlman 2013).

According to Buhlman, "If immediately after your death, you find yourself in a pleasant physical-like reflection of your past Earth environment, you are now standing within the astral dimension and far from your true spiritual home" (Buhlman 2016). He then advises you to recognize that your journey has just begun and that you have the creative ability to enhance your state of awareness and your resulting reality in the hereafter.

The next level is the most common level that people go to when they die, as it most closely resembles the vibrational frequency of Earth. Here we find people who actively transition, and also those who are recuperating from their time on Earth. There is an array of activities happening on this level. Activities here include deeper learning, as there is access to vast amounts of information and understanding. Many gravitate towards the activities they loved doing while on Earth, such as musicians playing in an orchestra, scientists working on projects, and others who are learning completely new skills. Some here choose to be a guide, helping those who are alive on Earth or helping those stuck in the intermediate zones to move on.

Most of the accounts from death experiences and communications from the deceased come from this level. There are descriptions of beautiful surroundings and breathtaking landscapes with fantastic, vibrant colors. Descriptions of things such as flowers emphasize hues that are far more vivid and striking than anything on Earth. The colors in the flowers seem alive as if they are made of moving energy. Water in streams, rivers, and lakes is described as shimmering with radiant light, as if the water is alive.

The people here are beautiful and helpful. There is no illness or aging of the physical body. Buildings in the cities are wonderful architectural structures that inspire and delight. Everything is peaceful, nothing is a problem, and everyone is happy. Most out-of-body experiences come from this level, as according to Jurgen Ziewe, "their physical consciousness draws them naturally to the environment that resembles our planet" (Ziewe 2008).

These are the traditional heavenly realms. At this level, you can manifest whatever you wish: fast cars, beautiful mansions, exquisite gardens, delicious food, and whatever other desire you may wish to fulfill. Whatever you seek is available, depending on your level of spiritual advancement. As you become more at one with yourself, you naturally align with the higher energies of the hereafter, unlocking greater creative power to shape your reality as you wish.

Ziewe met his father, who had died many years previously, on this level in the form of the young boy he had currently reincarnated as. His reincarnated father recognized him. This led him to believe that "on Higher Consciousness levels we have mature nonphysical bodies, which carry all the information from our past lives" (Ziewe 2015).

Ziewe recounts a pervading feeling of being "at home" in the higher dimensions. He describes "an incredible feeling of intimacy, of having been united with the truest feeling of 'home'." He goes on to say that "The higher a person ascends through the dimensions, the greater the power at their disposal. They also become more aware of an underlying intelligence, which permeates everything in the world around them" (Ziewe 2008). This intelligence keeps everything in motion throughout all dimensions.

The ascension through the higher realms is dependent on letting go of identification with the ego, and then letting go of any sense of identity, moving on to merging with Oneness. The apparent contradiction in all this is that the closer you get to completely letting go of all attachments, the closer you are to accessing your innermost self.

The light in the hereafter is often described as being different from that in the physical realm. It has been described as brighter, clearer, and more vibrant. As you move through the higher realms, there is an ever-increasing intensity in the level of light, which is somehow more familiar and comforting, once you have acclimatized to the vibration there.

The ultimate realms are often termed indescribable, because they are beyond the comprehension of the human mind and the capacity of our language to describe them. In these higher dimensions, there is little distinction between the creator and the created, as that which is created carries the imprint of its creator. Your thoughts at this level are created instantly and with great joy. So, while your thoughts create your reality in the hereafter, there is also a universal mind that is the universal collective consciousness acting as one, creating the infinite realms of existence.

The various realms are often divided by what has been described as a cloud or fog-like barrier. People can move through these barriers to go to a lower level if they choose. But one cannot pass through to a higher level unless one is accompanied by someone who can take one there.

Chapter 21

In between Lives

Michael Newton's research has contributed much to the accounts of what happens in the Spirit World between lives. Newton discovered in his hypnotherapy work that he could regress his clients to the Spirit World, where they were between earthly lives. Upon death, most go back to a spiritual home. Some do not accept the fact that their physical body is dead, and remain as what we call ghosts, until they are helped to move on. Those who have been traumatized by their earthly life usually go to a recuperation facility. Some who have been subverted by criminal abnormalities during their earthly life undergo separation at orientation and go into seclusion where they receive spiritual instruction to enable them to reintegrate with their hereafter group (Newton 1994).

Some of the first experiences after death are meeting your spiritual guide and having a life review. This review is not judgmental but is a process where there is reflection on your actions and the choices you made, and where you even feel the consequences of your actions on yourself and others. Then you meet the Council of Elders, which is a group of wise and advanced beings who help evaluate the lessons and experiences of your life and later assist you in choosing the most appropriate life path and lessons for your upcoming incarnation.

The Spirit World is described as a place of healing, rejuvenation, and learning, where you rejoin your group, comprised of others with whom you have a deep connection. Indeed you often reincarnate together in different roles to help each other learn and evolve.

According to Newton, there are several levels or groupings of souls in the hereafter. Beginner souls are souls that are young in terms of their experience of existence outside the Spirit World, and souls who have incarnated many times but remain immature. These souls tend to have simpler and less complex life experiences and may struggle with the basic concepts of morality, relationships, and personal growth.

Less developed souls tend to be stifled by a lack of independent thinking and are inclined to surrender their will to the controlling aspects of the culture and society in which they live. Such societies are often ones with a socio-economic structure that causes a large proportion of people to be subordinate to others. Beginner souls also lean towards being self-centered and do not easily accept others for who they are.

Every soul was once a beginner. Newton suggested that around 70 to 75 percent of the souls he regressed were in beginner or intermediate stages of development. Newton proposed that the more advanced souls who have gone through numerous lifetimes and gained deeper insights can choose to take on the role of teachers, healers, and guides to assist those in their earlier stages of development.

Intermediate souls have experienced and learned to navigate more complex situations and relationships. They often have experiences that teach them about love, trust, and mutual respect. They have developed empathy, are learning compassion, and are grappling with deeper moral and ethical questions. They are starting to recognize the interconnectedness of all beings and how their and others' actions have consequences for people around them.

They are learning not to be overly attached to material possessions and are seeking deeper spiritual understanding and clarity about their purpose, seeking jobs and roles where they can have the most positive impact. They are curious about the nature of reality and are often drawn to study philosophy, religion, or metaphysical concepts. They grow mainly through relationships, learning from their interactions with family, friends, partners, and even their apparent adversaries.

Intermediate souls are ready for more responsibilities, and their relationship with their guides changes to one of colleagues working together. They are learning how to be guides to younger souls, both in and out of physical incarnations. Not every soul becomes a guide, and those with different abilities and talents are given roles commensurate with their abilities.

Advanced souls, according to Newton, are scarce. In most cases, they are on Earth as incarnated guides who mostly go about their work in a quiet, unassuming manner. For themselves, they have mastered the fundamental issues most of us are wrestling with and are more interested in making small refinements on specific tasks for their advancement. Their fulfillment comes from improving the lives of other people.

They are recognized by their patience with society and the extraordinary coping skills they show, while their exceptional insight is most prominent. The advanced soul is found in all walks of life, but they are frequently in the helping professions. They radiate composure, kindness, and understanding towards others. They are not motivated by self-interest and may even disregard their own physical needs and live in reduced circumstances. All that being said, they may have some learning experiences that prompted them to reincarnate. Souls usually end their incarnations on Earth when they have reached full maturity.

The different levels or stages of existence in the hereafter through which you evolve are for learning about yourself and the nature of the universe, while refining your essence. The higher spiritual realms are characterized by greater levels of awareness, unity, and connection to universal consciousness, with which you ultimately merge in a state of oneness.

Tibetan Delogs

Further evidence of the after-death realms comes from the Tibetan "delogs," or "deloks," who are Tibetan people who have temporarily died and come back, often as a result of an illness. In Tibetan, *de-lok* means "returned from death." Their experiences lie somewhere between death experiences and shamanic journeying.

Delogs appear to be dead for several hours or even days, after which they revive spontaneously and recount details of their journey in the realms of the Tibetan otherworld. Delogs seem to penetrate much further into the realm of the hereafter than those who have death experiences. Delogs also bring back messages from departed loved ones. Many of these messages involve their supplications, reinforcing the basic message to change our lives while we are still alive in human form and have the opportunity to change.

One of the most famous, and relatively recent, delogs is Dawa Dhrolma, who died in 1941. Her story is recounted in her own words in the book *Delog: Journey to Realms beyond Death*. Afflicted by an illness, at the age of 16 she sought the opportunity, against the wishes of her spiritual teachers, to spend about five days in a deep meditative state, as if she were in a coma or in a state like death. She left specific instructions as to how she was to be looked after during this time. When she returned, she recounted the story of her experiences in the bardo. She became famous throughout Tibet (Dhrolma 2002).

Dhrolma describes encountering various deities, demons, and landscapes that represent different stages of the hereafter journey, consistent with the Buddhist teachings on the bardos. Her encounters can be interpreted in the context of manifestations of negative emotions and obstacles. Through her experiences, she conveys teachings about the impermanence of life, the importance of spiritual practice, and the karmic consequences of one's actions. The book gives insights into the Tibetan Buddhist cosmology and beliefs about death, dying, and the hereafter, including practices and rituals that guide individuals through these transitions.

In the introduction to the book *Delog: Journey to Realms beyond Death*, Chagdud Tulku Rinpoche says that

> Delog Dawa Drolma's account is as vivid as that of a tourist describing a country he or she has visited, yet hers is really a journey of consciousness through the pure and impure displays of mind. The delog experience is extraordinary, marvelous, even within the esoteric context of Tibetan schools of Vajrayana Buddhism. Yet Delog Dawa Drolma's account has the power and immediacy of direct experience, and I trust that those who read it will find that the phenomena of the realms correspond to aspects of their own mind's experience.
> (Dhrolma 2002)

Delving deeper into the realms and mysteries of the hereafter opens you up to creating new possibilities and options after your transition. The possibilities are endless. Whatever image of the hereafter that you have now developed is limited. There is always more to what you can imagine and visualize. You will have the most wonderful experience of the hereafter when you focus on love. When you look for love and look with love, when you hear with love, when you act with love, when you think with love, your hereafter will be filled with love and joy.

Chapter 22

Coming Back

Never again ... or maybe. There are many reasons why you might choose to come back to Earth to experience another lifetime, and many reasons why you might not. At some point, when you are in the Spirit World, you may begin to wonder about the possible benefits of another earthly life. The decision to return to Earth is not always an easy one, as leaving the beautiful, peaceful environment of the Spirit World can be difficult. Yet the desire to experience more on the physical plane, to grow more, or to help others, can hold a strong appeal.

Physical life has many attractions that can cause us to consider returning. The many physical sensations that you experience, from satiating your hunger, fulfilling sexual desires, to the simple pleasures of being hugged or relaxing and enjoying life, are all to be found here on Earth. Only in the physical environment of Earth can you experience such things as the warmth of the sun on your skin, the sensation of walking along the seashore, or the wind blowing on your face.

The choice to have another life on Earth may be to bring new information or a new invention for the benefit of humanity. You may wish to come back to be part of creating something new, to bring through new ways of being, or of doing something differently. You may choose to come back to be of service to others in a myriad of ways that are possible here on Earth.

So, despite the times of physical and emotional pain that you experienced in a previous life, and may be experiencing in this lifetime, there is much to attract you back and things that you may wish to experience again. The main reason for returning is to further your spiritual growth; to learn to love more.

Selection of your forthcoming life on Earth and its experiences is done with great care and consideration, with input from advanced guides and others in your hereafter group. This happens first in what Newton calls the "place of life selection," where several possible lives are shown, each with its learnings and opportunities. This place is described as being like a movie theatre with banks of screens where you can view yourself in the future, in a wide variety of roles in many different settings.

Each of these lives can be tried out, although all aspects of these lives cannot be experienced, as choices made during the time on Earth can change the outcome in later years. Before leaving this life-selection area, you will have selected one scenario for your next incarnation on Earth. The events of the planned and chosen life are not all predestined. Rather, you are choosing a set of life events and circumstances perfectly planned by you. Yet the outcomes of these life events are open-ended depending on the choices made during the lifetime.

One of the first selections for the next life is the location where that life will be experienced. Then, choices are made regarding race and culture, which involve your choice of parents. Depending on the life experiences you have chosen, members of your group will agree to be your parents and play the role required for your experiences and learning. Others involved in your life plan are also pursuing their own life plan in a highly complex interrelationship overseen by overarching consciousness.

Great care is taken in choosing the right body to experience the next incarnation. You choose a female or male body, and the physical attributes you wish to have, including whether or not to experience some disability. Most choices are made with a view to having different experiences from previous lives to enable further spiritual evolution.

When all decisions about incarnating are made, the preparation stage begins. This is like cramming for a final exam, where you go to what is commonly called the "place of recognition." Before embarking on the journey to the physical once again, you go before the Council of Elders for a second time, who reinforce the significance of your choices for the next life. Some return one last time to their group to say their last goodbyes, while others go straight to the embarkation place. This is the last time you enjoy the knowledge of who you are before you must adapt to being in a new body.

Once you make the choice, you then have the knowledge of all that went with it taken from you so that you can learn without foreknowledge. Yet you also retain a certain sense of purpose and direction in life. This can present itself as a strong feeling that there is something that you are supposed to do, and that subtly tells you when you are off course. There are also pointers planted in your subconscious that trigger when you come across a certain situation or person in life that is significant for your learning. This is often experienced as a sense of "déjà vu" or a sense of knowing this person or place from before.

Choosing a new life on Earth also involves deciding how much of your core spiritual energy you bring with you. Michael Newton observed that you bring a certain percentage of your total energy with you when you incarnate. The rest remains in the hereafter to guide and watch what you are doing, providing help with managing physical life, even if you are unaware of its presence and assistance. It is there when you die to be the pure essence with which you reconnect as you return to the hereafter.

Newton recorded from his clients that the average less-advanced soul will put between 50 and 75 percent into a physical body, whereas more advanced souls will never transfer more than 25 percent. According to information learned through life-between-life sessions, Newton says that with the help of your guides, you choose as far as possible a life that will have some challenges for you to go through and help you grow, but one that is not too much for the amount of soul energy that you are bringing through (Newton 1994).

When everything about your next incarnation has been decided, you are ready to reinhabit a physical body. Everything is put in place for your conception, your time in the womb, and the place and time of birth. It is no accident where and when you are born, even if your birth appears to have been induced or premature. You may choose to enter the womb at conception or may move in and out of the fetus during the pregnancy. Your birth into this physical life is commensurate with your temporary death from the world of spirit.

At some point in your cycles of living and dying in the physical realm of Earth, you will decide that there is no more for you to learn or experience on the earthly plane. Your focus will shift to other realms and opportunities to have different experiences and be a part of the ever-expanding consciousness.

Chapter 23

Death Training Camp

Practice makes perfect. The thought of training for death or preparing for death is alien to many people. At present, much of humanity's understanding of death is that you are helpless, powerless, and a reluctant participant in what is happening. The consideration that you can be an active participant in this wonderful and amazing transition of consciousness is beyond the bounds of many people's current awareness. Yet, when you actively seek to know everything you can about death and prepare yourself for an informed transition, you are empowering yourself, reducing the fear of death, and even moving towards a place of loving death.

As a spiritual being, you trained and prepared for your incarnation in the physical body that you now occupy. Just as you studied, observed, and chose the aspects of your current life, you can also study and prepare for your death transition back to the Spirit World and influence what experiences you have there.

The adage "Fail to prepare and you prepare to fail" applies equally to death as to life. Failure in death is not widely considered because the fact that death comes to everyone at some point leads many to believe that you do not influence the outcome of this event. There are many ways to die. A successful death involves being as knowledgeable and informed as possible so that you know what to expect and have practiced as many aspects of it as you can. Diligent and ongoing preparation for your death sets the stage for a more successful and harmonious transition.

In training for death and the hereafter, it is important to learn as much as you can about the death event and the transition of your consciousness. The Spirit World is not way out there somewhere. It is all around you, and also deep within you. When you travel to the farthest reaches of the universe and go to your deepest inner depths, you find the same place. Your spiritual path lies within you. Dag Hammerskjold, former Secretary General of the United Nations, said: "The longest journey is the journey inwards." Your journey at death and after death is a journey inwards to the core of your being.

There are many ways to train for death. Some of them you can choose to practice, while others appear to happen uninvited. Dreams are a great training ground to explore and prepare for your death. Jurgen Ziewe writes that "with every experience in ever higher dimensions, the thing that I began to appreciate most of all was that dreams and the next dimensions are closely related" (Ziewe 2008). He suggests that some training could change our awareness of our dreams with results of extraordinary potential.

Dreams are a connection between your physical reality and your spiritual reality. The connections between your dream world and your everyday world are not always obvious. Your physical world provides much of the information for what happens in dreams, but the experiences take place in your consciousness. As your consciousness is much larger and diverse than you currently know, your dreams are when your inner consciousness enters a parallel dream reality and creates experiences there. While all experiences take place in your consciousness, it is not always clear how what is happening in your physical everyday reality is happening in your consciousness.

Dreams give you a glimpse of how other realities operate. In the realms of the hereafter, just as in dreams, things can change very rapidly. These changes are always in response to your thoughts and wishes, although it is not always obvious that you are the creator of what you are experiencing. Dreams and death both reflect life. The spiritual energies, forces, and beings that you encounter in dreams and death correspond to those you are connected with in your waking life. Dreams and death are merely shifts in the subtle dimensions of your consciousness.

Your dreams represent the state of your consciousness and your level of awareness. They bring repressed emotions, memories, and archetypes to the surface, revealing aspects of awareness that may be hidden during wakefulness. Dreams mainly communicate through symbols and metaphors, revealing subconscious beliefs and fears. They often link personal experiences to broader spiritual or universal themes. In essence, dreams map the spectrum of awareness, from immediate emotional needs to existential truths, by combining conscious experiences, unconscious material, and archetypal wisdom. Their complexity reflects the depth of your emotional awareness and your capacity for self-reflection, healing, and growth.

In training for death, recording and examining your dreams gives you insights into your state of consciousness. You usually have four to six dreams per night over a two-hour period. Most people do not remember all of them, and even the memory of dramatic-type dreams can fade quickly if not recorded. One way to help remember where you go in your dreams is to keep a dream journal. Diligently writing down what you experienced in your dreams leads to you becoming better at remembering your next dreams. When you have a written record of your dreams, you can begin to identify and examine common themes and occurrences that prompt you to become more aware of different states of consciousness. As you become better at remembering your dreams, you can move to a place of becoming aware of the fact that you are dreaming, often referred to as "lucid dreaming."

Lucid dreaming is a proactive form of dreaming where you first become aware that you are dreaming while you are dreaming. It involves the ability to shift your center of awareness into a higher state and intentionally enter more elevated planes of existence. When you become aware of being lucid in your dreams, you can then begin to create what you choose to experience in your dreams. Aspects of lucid dreaming can include astral travel and remote viewing.

Lucid dreaming is similar to how you can operate in the realms of the hereafter. Just as you can create your reality and carry out activities in your lucid dreams, you can also choose to create your life in the hereafter. If you have not experienced lucid dreaming, you can improve your chances of it through training and practice.

Training in lucid dreaming involves a few key practices to increase the likelihood of becoming aware and in control within your dreams. You can do what is commonly called "reality checks" during the day, where you ask yourself, "Am I dreaming?" The practice of checking a clock for the time, then looking away and checking it again to see if it has changed dramatically or behaves normally, is a good reality check. Another practice is to jump upwards to see if you can defy the laws of gravity. In a lucid dream, you can jump as high as you wish. Doing these or other practices regularly makes them a habit that you can carry over into your dreams as dream reality checks.

Other practices for lucid dreaming training include repeating a phrase before you go to sleep, such as "I will realize that I am dreaming," as it sets the intention to become lucid in your dreams. The practice of getting up and going back to bed after four to six hours of sleep increases your chances of entering a "rapid eye movement" (REM) phase where lucid dreaming is most likely to happen. Visualization, such as seeing yourself becoming lucid in a recent dream and imagining what you would do, reinforces the idea of becoming aware that you are dreaming. With regular practice, these and other techniques help to improve the likelihood of achieving a lucid dream.

You can also train for and experience states outside the body. According to the many accounts from out-of-body travelers, it is possible to visit the Spirit World during these travels. Exploring the Spirit World in out-of-body travels can help prepare you for where your consciousness goes after death. Even if you do not experience out-of-body traveling, reading about the various accounts of the hereafter by other out-of-body travelers can help you prepare for and visualize what you can expect after death. Indeed, reading and watching videos about all aspects of death and the hereafter can help bring you to a new understanding and realization of who you are and what death involves.

One of the most common and straightforward ways of training for death is through the practice of meditation. Meditation is a wonderful way to explore your thoughts, feelings, and even actions around your death. One approach to meditation is finding the point of stillness within you and resting there for as long as you can through whatever thoughts come and go, and in whatever situations present themselves. Jurgen Ziewe is certain that without meditation, none of his out-of-body experiences would have occurred (Ziewe 2008). He also says that "Meditation, which focuses attention away from the outside world of our senses, away from our conditioned mind and thoughts, is the only way to break away from the old and embrace new and unknown realms of consciousness" (Ziewe 2015).

Meditation on impermanence is an approach to your death where you contemplate the inevitability of death and the fact that, at some stage, the physical body dies. As you contemplate the impermanence of the physical body, you also meditate on the transfer of consciousness and your state of awareness in the moments immediately before, during, and after the death of the body.

The act of contemplating death and being reminded of mortality has been a significant practice across numerous cultures and societies. In Ancient Greece and Rome, philosophers such as Socrates and the Stoics advocated for contemplating one's death as a means to living more authentically and fully. In Buddhist practice, some monks have historically meditated in cemeteries or among corpses to confront the impermanence of life and reduce attachment to the physical world. Similarly, Hindu *Aghori* activities are deeply centered on contemplating death. Their rituals, such as living in cremation grounds, meditating on corpses, and using human remains are designed to confront mortality directly, embrace the impermanence of life, and transcend fear and attachment associated with death.

The concept of *Memento mori* (Latin for "Remember death" or "Remember that you die") is an artistic or symbolic reminder of the inevitability of death that has its roots in Christianity and features in art from the medieval period onwards. It often includes images of skulls and skeletons as reminders of death.

The Buddhist practice of *mananasati* (mindfulness of death) is a practice of frequently keeping in mind that death can strike at any time. *Mananasati* also includes various visualizations and contemplation techniques to meditate on the nature of death. *Memento mori*, *mananasati*, and other contemplations on death initially appear fear-based and focused on the physical demise and decomposition of the body, rather than the focus being on you as a loving spiritual being. The concept of being aware of death on an everyday basis can also be found in the Bible in Paul's first letter to the Corinthians, chapter 15, verse 31, where he writes, "I die daily."

When you contemplate your death on a regular basis from a place of love, it keeps you focused on yourself as a spiritual being and leads to an enhanced understanding of life and all its happenings. The practice of living actively with death, of dying before you die, brings a vibrancy to your life. It shifts and softens the perceived division between this life and the hereafter. Contemplating death changes your life as you live.

When you face your death regularly, you are practicing symbolic dying before you die. Then, when death comes, you are ready. You are more than ready; you are welcoming it. You are welcoming the beautiful and amazing shift in your consciousness and awareness with deep and sincere joy.

Conscious dying is the practice of using the dying process as an opportunity to be more present and loving, and more conscious of your eternal spiritual nature. The process encourages living fully in the present, letting go of attachments, and embracing death as a natural part of life. Conscious dying practices have the twofold purpose of preparing you for imminent death and also transforming how you live.

Awareness of Consciousness Levels

There are many levels of consciousness of which you can be aware, knowledge of which can be training for your death. You will most likely have experienced some of these already in your life. Bob Monroe of the Monroe Institute and others have mapped certain levels of consciousness, which they name "Focus Levels." For example, Focus One is normal waking consciousness, and Focus Ten is the state of "Mind awake, body asleep," which is a state of deep physical relaxation with alert awareness. Monroe also describes phases of awareness such as full waking consciousness, daydreaming, meditation, and other hypnagogic states, hypnotic states, alcohol- and drug-induced states, dreams, lucid dreams, spontaneous out-of-body states, death experiences, coma, controlled out-of-body states, and more.

William Buhlman has written about his out-of-body experiences in his books, including *Adventures in the Afterlife* and *The Secret of the Soul*. He says that "Out-of-body experiences are exciting because they provide personal proof of our immortality, firsthand observations of the nonphysical universe, and a glimpse of our future spiritual home" (Buhlman 2001).

Buhlman goes on to write that the profound act of projecting your consciousness beyond the body can have an immediate and life-changing impact, dramatically confirming your immortality and allowing you to experience yourself in a shocking new light. He says that "Out-of-body explorers simply do not fear death. They fully understand that death is a natural and exciting transition of consciousness. They have a tremendous advantage over the fearful masses that cling to the density of the flesh" (Buhlman 2001). Along with many other advantages, OBEs also provide invaluable insights into the nature of our multidimensional spiritual selves, allowing us to experience and adapt to the thought-responsive realities we will enter after death (Buhlman 2013).

In his book *Adventures Beyond the Body*, Buhlman recounts an encounter with his deceased uncle (Buhlman 1996). After Buhlman left his body, he moved into the living room of his house and was surprised when someone called his name from the couch. It was his deceased uncle, Hilton. His conversation with his Uncle Hilton convinced him that it is obvious that we continue after death. What also struck him was that his uncle was in the prime of his life, rather than being an overweight 54-year-old as he was when he died. Buhlman considers that "it seems likely that after we shed our physical body at death, we assume the energy form molded or influenced by our concept of ourselves."

Be aware that you are not alone in your exploration. Just as you have guides and guardian angels watching over you every moment of every day, you also have a guide with you in your dreams, meditations, and out-of-body explorations. It is not uncommon for someone to sense the presence of someone else with them in an ordinary dream. Oftentimes, the identity of this dream companion is not clear at the time, but you know that they are there. Assistance is always available to you in whatever state you find yourself, but it must be requested.

Consciousness exploration and death training are about informing yourself as much as you can of what to expect and what awaits you after death. Practicing one or more of the death trainings is a life-enhancing and death-enhancing approach and can have a profound and liberating effect on your life and death.

Continuing to research death and incorporating death practices into your everyday life reinforces the belief that life does not end at the death of your physical body. The deeper your contemplation of your death, the more exciting the prospect of setting out on the great journey of your death becomes. While advanced out-of-body experiences and lucid dreaming travels appear to offer some of the deepest insights into the nonphysical realms, dreams and meditation are more easily accessible and are powerful practices for exploring your death and the hereafter.

Death-Training Exercise

One powerful death-training practice is to walk or finger trace a labyrinth with your focus on your death. Physically walking a labyrinth is recommended. This is best done with someone you trust and who you can rely on to support you, such as a trained facilitator or a trained counselor who has experience of working with the labyrinth or death.

This is a deep practice that you need to be able to carry out in a safe and undisturbed environment. You are seeking to experience, on a theoretical and energetic level, the death of the physical body that you now occupy.

In summary, you walk the labyrinth starting at the entrance, representing where you now are in your life. The walk in represents your life from now until your death. The center represents the moment of your physical death. The walk back out of the labyrinth is about you coming back into the world with new awareness of the place of death in your life.

The Training

At the entrance of the labyrinth, picture yourself as you are now in your life. Begin walking, and as you walk, see in your mind all the dreams, hopes, and thoughts that you have for the future. Work through all the things that you would like to do while you are here on Earth. When you have gone through everything that you want to do, see where you are in the labyrinth. Are you near the center? Take a mental note for later of the place where you feel that you have fulfilled all your life's work.

If you are not close to the center of the labyrinth, slowly make your way to just before the center of the labyrinth. At the point where you enter the center of the labyrinth, imagine what it would be like for you to leave your physical body, or for your physical body to fade away and be no more. If you can, lie down in the center of the labyrinth and lie still. If you feel comfortable doing so, close your eyes. Again, visualize what it would be like for you to no longer have a physical body.

Preferably with your eyes closed, allow your thoughts and consciousness to take you where they will. As far as possible, keep your mind clear of what is happening, what might be happening, and any judgment of what is happening. Stay in a state of awareness and observation, noting what you are feeling and sensing.

When your thoughts return to your physical body, focus on being fully present in your body. Keep your eyes closed for a short while longer, and when you feel ready, open your eyes. Allow yourself time to readjust to your surroundings, to being in a physical body. Feel your presence in every part of your body: your head, your torso, your legs, your feet and toes, your arms and hands. Feel the aliveness in your whole body. Allow yourself plenty of time to come back to being fully present in the body. Slowly rise and get ready to make your way out of the labyrinth. The walk back out of the labyrinth is about you coming back into the world with new awareness.

Reflecting on the Training

Immediately after the walk, write down any thoughts that came to you during any aspect of this walk, and particularly while in the center where you visualized yourself leaving your physical body.

Write about how you felt during the walk. Write about what thoughts came to you, particularly when you were in the center. Write about any fears that came up for you. Write about the people who came to mind during the walk.

Write a few sentences about how you now feel about the death of the physical body. Consider what you might do differently in your life, and in preparation for your death.

Chapter 24

Death Wish

Your death wish is your escape plan. It is your plan for liberation from the physical. It includes detailed instructions for you and for others to be fulfilled before, during, and after your time of transition from your physical body. Creating your death escape plan applies more to a death where you have some control over where and how you will transition, such as dying in a bed at home or in a care setting.

In the event of a sudden and unexpected death due to an accident or catastrophe, much of what follows will not apply, although what you learn between now and then about death and dying will inform how you make your transition. The preparation and training will help you know better what is happening and enable you to choose how you wish to be.

Some deaths by accident or misadventure can result in the person being kept alive or on life support for some time. You most likely will not be conscious but may have some awareness of your condition and what is happening around you. In those circumstances, having prescribed your wishes in advance can be both a comfort and support as the moment of your death nears.

The more specific you can be in your death wish, the better. Write down everything you can about the arrangements you would like at your dying and death. Create detailed instructions that you wish to be carried out when you may no longer have the physical capabilities to do so, or you wish to focus fully on your state of being.

Your death is a special and precious moment. The more support you have around you, the easier and more successful your death will be. Select the people who will support and assist you in this part of your spiritual plan. If you can, choose one person to be your Anam Cara, or Soul Friend, who will be with you as much as possible and whom you trust to make the best decisions for you when you may no longer be able.

You may wish to engage a death doula or death midwife to assist you in the dying process. A death doula is a specialist person who can perform a range of services, including creating death plans and providing spiritual, psychological, and social support before, during, and just after death.

Make your Anam Cara or death doula fully aware of all your death wishes. You will need to have gone through every aspect of your death transition with them, so they are fully informed about your wishes. Some factors to consider include who to have in the room, how you would like the room set up, and any private thoughts or concerns you have.

Central to a smooth transition is the creation of a sacred space from which you will transition from your physical body. Create a sacred atmosphere in the room by including things that will support and inspire you during your transition. Indicate the level and type of lighting you would like to have. Consider if you would like to have an altar with images of deities, spiritual teachers, and others whose images uplift you and represent the flow of love. You may wish to have images of sacred symbols, such as the Om (the sound of creation) or the flower of life, or other items that have a special meaning for you and are visible to you.

If you want to have music played, then choose music that is of a high frequency and is supportive of a calm and centered state of mind. It may be soothing instrumental music, sacred chants, or hymns. If you have recorded some affirmations to have spoken as your time nears, give guidance to your Anam Cara as to how you think you might wish these to be interspersed with the music. If there is one affirmation or phrase that you wish repeated frequently, indicate this in advance.

Examples of affirmations include "I unite fully with my spiritual self," "I am Love," and "I reunite fully with Source." The Buddhist affirmation and instruction "Go to the clear light of the void" is a particularly powerful message to hear as you transition. A simple yet profound one is "Love and be loved." If you are looking for other suggestions, William Buhlman recommends over 50 affirmations in his book *Adventures in the Afterlife*. You can incorporate your affirmations into your everyday life, so they are second nature to you.

Setting out in advance how you expect to be as the moment of your death nears can be both instructive for those present and reassuring for you. While you may not know exactly how you will be, consideration in advance of how you expect to be and feel is a core part of death training and your death wishes.

As you near your moment of death, keep your focus and attention on your ultimate spiritual destination. In the moments of separating from the physical body, keep focused on your highest intention, and stay in a state of detachment from the physical material world. Fix your awareness on whatever level of consciousness you wish to attain upon death. The lure of the physical can be strong, and the attractiveness of a similar realm in the hereafter can have a comforting appeal. This is the time to hold firm to your intention of achieving as high a spiritual state as possible.

It can also be comforting to meet, or seek to meet, loved ones who have already passed. Yet, when met by loved ones at death, according to Buhlman:

> few ever stop to question this wonderful reunion process and most assume that this is the only option available to them. However, when we explore deeper, we awaken to a startling truth; during this joyful reunification with loved ones we have unknowingly accepted and merged our

> state of consciousness with the vibrational energies and consensus limits of [the] loved one's collective reality. (Buhlman 2016)

So, hold firm your intention of achieving as high a spiritual state as possible. You can always visit deceased relatives later on at your choosing.

Have in the room the people who are familiar with your intentions, supporting you during your transition and reminding you of your spiritual destination. This room does not have to be open to everyone who knows you or to every family member. Let family and friends know who you are choosing to accompany you during this time. This is your special time. Everybody and anybody, including family members, does not have the right to be there. You can ask those not present to hold a loving space as best they can wherever they are.

Request those present to focus on your spiritual being rather than your physical body. While the body may need some tending to, keep this to a minimum. Ask those present to see you for the spiritual energy that is inhabiting the body and about to leave the body. Know that this is not an ending but a transition to another state of consciousness.

Request those who are present at your transition to be comfortable with your death; to be at ease with themselves as you leave the body. The greater their comfort with the dying process, the more vividly they will perceive the awe-inspiring and graceful transition as you leave the body, and the more intimately they will share in this wondrous spiritual event.

You can indicate that you would like those present to stay with your remains and continue to provide guidance and encouragement to you after you have left the body, holding the high-vibrational energy of the sacred space for as long as your Anam Cara considers necessary. You can also specify, in your death wishes, what others are to do if you leave the body in an unexpected or sudden way. You can request that the people you have asked to be present pause and hold space for you, knowing that you have chosen this means of making the transition for your own reasons, whatever they may be. If you have specific wishes for your remains after your death, then spell these out to your loved ones who will be carrying them out.

The type of funeral arrangements can impact some people's transition. In the chapter on grief, we have heard how mourning and grieving can keep the deceased person more focused on and even bound to the physical earthly realm. In some traditions, it is considered that the person who has died may stay close to the dead body for several days, often until the funeral is finished. The deceased person can wait around to see how their loved ones are doing. They can be very aware of what is happening at the funeral ceremony, so focusing on the deceased person can be helpful and supportive.

Funeral arrangements and rituals are important in supporting the transition of the person who has died. Some current funeral practices do not necessarily serve the needs of the deceased or the best interests of those still alive on Earth. Many funeral practices are long-standing, ingrained, and performed out of habit rather than having an intended energetic benefit. Furthermore, there is also little consideration given to the power, intentions, and collective energy of everyone present at the funeral, which can be an immense source of support for the recently deceased. A new approach is called for.

A Funeral for Life

A "funeral for life" is one where funerals are about life and about loving the role that death plays in the game of life. Present-day funerals mainly operate on the incorrect assumption that the dead body is the person. As mentioned several times, you are not your body, either in death or in life. Consideration needs to be given to treating the dead body with dignity and respect and honoring the role that it played in the life of the person, but this is not the main aim of the new funeral. Also, while the bereaved are to be considered, the primary consideration is on the person who has passed.

The purposes of the funeral for life are manifold. It places the focus and attention on the new state of existence of the person who has passed. Switching the focus away from the physical and onto the spiritual energy of the person helps the bereaved to be aware of their loved one's continued presence. Not having the dead body on display encourages attendees to connect with the essence or energy of the person, now existing in a different dimension. This supports the development of a new, primarily energetic relationship, benefiting both the living and the departed.

The funeral for life provides guidance and support to the person who has passed into the hereafter. Cremation is a wonderful way of breaking bonds with the physical world. The act of scattering the ashes is a symbolic indication that you now exist in a different dimension.

Ashes can be shared with the five elements of earth, air, fire, water, and the fifth element of spirit. Sprinkle some ashes into clear seawater. Spread some on the ground at sacred sites. Scatter the ashes to the four winds at locations of your choosing. As the ashes are scattered to the elements, know that this is a symbolic act recognizing that the energy of the deceased exists everywhere: in the breath of the air, on the ground of the earth, in the waters of the rivers and seas, in the food that is eaten, and in every thought of the one who is now elsewhere.

After breaking bonds with the physical, conveying messages telepathically to the person who has passed can help them navigate the realms of the hereafter. Rituals and ceremonies that assist them in transitioning, such as lighting a candle or prayer-type ceremonies, act as metaphoric bridges, signaling to the deceased person that their earthly journey has ended.

Buddhists have many practices, such as praying, chanting, and reading from the *Book of the Dead*. Other religions have a practice of reciting prayers for the soul of the deceased in the hereafter. The deeper your understanding of the hereafter, the more fully you can serve and be of assistance to those who dwell within its realms. The bereaved can also help and support the one who has passed through prayers, heartfelt intentions for their well-being, and requesting higher spiritual beings to assist them.

Another purpose of the funeral for life is to transform the relationship between the bereaved and the deceased. After-death relationships involve adjusting to a new reality. By bridging the tangible and intangible, rituals help transform the sense of loss into a feeling of continuity enabling the living to integrate this new connection into their lives. Practices that foster a calm state of mind, such as meditation, mindfulness, labyrinth walking, recording dreams, or speaking to the deceased in a meaningful setting, can support this adjustment. These activities not only promote inner peace but can also facilitate ongoing communication with loved ones who have passed. Seeking out messages and signs from the recently deceased provides opportunities for the deceased to make contact more easily.

The funeral for life is an honoring and a celebration of the person who has passed. Just as their birthdays were celebrated, their deathday is also a time for celebration. Evidence from those who have communicated from the hereafter is that they present themselves in the prime of their lives, not as they were when they left the body. Having friends and family bring photos and memories of the person in their prime, or how they best remember them, helps to establish a healthy ongoing relationship.

The ultimate aim of the funeral for life is to create a feeling of wellness and joy for both the bereaved and the deceased. Consider dispensing with some of the current practices of mourning. You could ask everyone to wear brightly colored clothes, or all white, or even fancy dress costume. Play upbeat music and make the funeral a celebration, not a funeral. Dance to music that is full of life.

The death celebration is for the person who has passed. Its essence can be summed up in the words of Elisabeth Kübler-Ross, who told her children: "When I die, release balloons in the sky to celebrate that I graduated. For me, death is a graduation" (Grimes 2010). The funeral for life is an honoring of the person's current life in a new state of being. Know that they are not only watching but are present and enjoying the celebration.

Chapter 25

Happy Deathday

You were born to die. Your birthday is your deathday. If you were not born, you would not die. We celebrate birthdays to acknowledge our coming into the world. Yet we mostly avoid the fact that birthdays are a reminder that leaving this world is inevitable. As you age, you become increasingly aware that your lifespan in this body is limited. Some people avoid celebrating their birthday as it is a reminder for them that their body is getting older and will, at some stage, be no more.

Life is to be celebrated. Death as a continuation of life is also to be celebrated. Avoiding celebration diminishes your life force. Taking every opportunity to celebrate life makes you feel more alive. When you celebrate death, you become even more alive as you are celebrating your infinite nature that will exist when the physical body is no more.

Changing your birthday to your "deathday" is an act of recognizing the beauty and the celebratory nature of birth and death. Each year on the anniversary of your birth, hold a deathday celebration. Bake a deathday cake and light a candle to represent the light within you that will move on to another dimension after this body ceases to be. Ask people to send you deathday wishes and deathday cards. Becoming comfortable with your death brings great joy and a more vibrant approach to life. In the words of the Roman philosopher Lucius Annaeus, "The day which we fear as our last is but the birthday of eternity."

Invite friends to come and participate in the celebrations. Have them sing a "Happy Deathday" song to celebrate your comings and goings into and from this lifetime:

Happy Deathday to you,

Happy Deathday to you,
Happy Deathday, dear ...
Happy Deathday to you.

If celebrating your deathday on your birthday is too much of a jump for you at the moment, then you can choose another day on which to celebrate your death. That way, you get to have two celebrations of your existence in one year. Choose a day that you think would be a good day to die. You could choose an auspicious day in your culture's calendar, such as one of the Celtic festivals of light or Diwali, an Asian lantern festival day, the winter solstice, or any day that appeals to you. If you are brave enough, you can also choose the year. Given that the average lifespan in the Western world is around 80 years, choose a year between 80 and 90 years from your birth year and see that as your death year. If you are already over 90 years old, use your imagination.

As you read this, you may feel the closeness of your death. Feelings of anxiety, dread, and fear may arise as you consider choosing a year in which to die. These feelings are to be welcomed. Once you become aware of them, you can focus on them, feel the fear, and do it anyway. And in recognizing the emotions that you have about death, you can choose to change any that are not love. In doing so, you are taking another step towards loving death.

A happy death follows a happy life. To be in a position to look forward to and celebrate your death, you may wish to consider making some adjustments to how you live your life. You can find inspiration from poets, mystics, artists, playwrights, and spiritual teachers who have often touched on the happiness in death. Leonardo da Vinci said: "As a well-spent day brings happy sleep, so a life well used brings happy death," while Mahatma Gandhi advised: "Live as if you were to die tomorrow. Learn as if you were to live forever." Mark Twain wrote that "the fear of death follows from the fear of life. A man who lives fully is prepared to die at any time."

Focusing on a happy death helps create a happy death. Adopting a celebratory attitude to death will bring you closer to having a joyous death as you enter another dimension on your journey. Celebrating the death of a person is celebrating them being born into their new way of being. Celebrating your death is a gift to yourself, and also a gift to humanity in challenging and changing society's attitudes to death.

As you will not be around in physical form to enjoy the celebrations of your passing, do it now. Organize your death party. If you are not sure about celebrating your deathday on your own, join with a friend and celebrate both your deaths on the same day. You could even organize a party where everyone attending celebrates their deathday. How much fun would that be?

"Deathday" is a rarely used word. It is so rare that it doesn't show up on Microsoft Word spellcheck. However, it is found in some English dictionaries. According to Dictionary.com (2025), "deathday" means "the day or the anniversary of the day of a person's death." The deathday we are talking about here is different, as it is celebrated in anticipation of your death rather than in remembrance of it.

Your deathday is the first day of the rest of your life. Your deathday is today. Your deathday is every day. When you fully grasp your deathday concept, it can stop you in your tracks and cause you to pause and consider how you choose to be today. And the ultimate choice is love.

Choose to love today. Choose to love everything that is happening. Choose to love every moment of today and every day. And have fun with what you choose. Experience the joy of life and the joy of death. And when you are fully comfortable with your deathday, choose to share your comfort with others. For you are sharing love. You are choosing love over fear. You are choosing to see death as it is meant to be seen: as a shift in awareness and existence; as your doorway to freedom; as the greatest gift of the meaning of life.

Just as birthdays are a recognition of the passing of time, deathdays are a recognition of transcending time. Time is a concept here in the physical world. The more you are focused on time, the less you know and understand about your timeless nature. Celebrating your forthcoming death is a reminder that life always exists; that it just changes form. So, celebrate your death. Happy Deathday to you.

Chapter 26

Death — Wanted Alive

There is life in death. But you have to look for it. When you find it, you have tapped into the wellspring of eternal life. You are alive when you have the awareness that life cannot end. You are alive when you know that you cannot die. You are alive when you know that you exist before your birth and exist after your death.

The shift in awareness from fear of death to loving death involves moving from seeing death as the end to seeing death as a continuation of life. This mindset transformation does not just happen; it must be sought and lived. Doing nothing, or continuing to be oblivious to your ongoing nature, is a recipe for a dying life and an unlived death.

If you take life for granted or if you consider that "this is just the way it is," then you will experience a similar way of being in the hereafter. When you take where you are in the hereafter for granted, you will be unaware of the infinite possibilities that are available to you there, just as you are here on Earth.

If you die today, you move in the hereafter to the same vibrational frequency at which you now resonate. This knowledge brings a responsibility that many tend to avoid or not recognize. It may be easier not to accept that your future is in your hands because your present is in your hands.

Your life here on Earth is part of the greater flow of life that you are. Death is also a part of this flow of life. Death is the part of life that shifts your consciousness from one form to another: from consciousness within physical form to consciousness without physical attachments. Death can only be understood fully when the purpose of life is also recognized.

Life on Earth is about your evolution. It is about evolving as a human and spiritual being through experiencing new and sometimes challenging circumstances in a relatively safe environment. It is about recognizing yourself as a spiritual being living as a human being with infinite potential as part of the one consciousness. Earth is an ideal environment where you can learn to play the game of life.

In life, everything exists. You always have and always will exist. Non-existence, by its very description, cannot exist. You cannot not exist. Your existence requires you to be aware of your aliveness and to live your life in the knowing that death is a part of being alive. Death is a part of aliveness, and your realization of this brings death to life.

The truth for many is their perspective of the events that happen in their lives. These are perceived truths born from preconceived thoughts and ideas of how things are. Change your perception, and your truth changes. Observing from a place of non-judgment and love opens doors to greater truth. When you free yourself from the relative truth of your former narrow perceptions, you are open to the absolute truth of existence.

The energy on Earth is dense and slow-moving in comparison to the higher realms you experience in the hereafter. William Buhlman considers that Earth is a learning environment, what he calls "a slowed-down molecular training ground of consciousness." It is a dense realm of matter, where focused thoughts are required in order to create and prosper. It is an ideal environment where the young and undisciplined mind can learn by trial and error without contaminating the pure realm of spirit (Buhlman 2001).

An alternative viewpoint is put forward by Bashar, an extraterrestrial entity who is from a parallel universe, specifically from a civilization that exists hundreds of years in the future. Bashar, channeled by Daryl Anka, considers that we are all mature souls who have chosen to come to Earth at this time to have experiences that will bring this lifetime more into alignment with how life in the hereafter is experienced (Bashar

Communications Inc. 2025). In effect, this life is about creating a vibration here on Earth that is similar to your true vibration in the hereafter and creating Heaven here on Earth.

The souls that come to Earth are highly unique and have chosen to incarnate here for specific reasons tied to personal growth, learning, and experience. Bashar emphasizes that Earth is a very specific and challenging environment, and the souls who come here are considered particularly advanced and courageous due to the intensity of the physical and emotional experiences that they face.

Buhlman says that the effectiveness and speed by which thought energy restructures an energy environment is determined by the intensity of the thought and the density of the energy it is acting upon (Buhlman 2001). On Earth, because of its dense environment, great intensity of thought is required to change the energy. This has many advantages in that your thoughts do not automatically and immediately manifest in your life and change your environment. The dense energy means that the effect of your thoughts on the world around you is not immediately obvious. Yet, when you look back over time, you can see where your thoughts and intentions brought about changes in your life. Your thoughts and intentions from the past brought you to where you are now.

An essential requirement of your current reality is mastering the ability to carefully choose and focus your thoughts. When you take time to consider everything in your life, some of the connections start to become clear. Once you realize that your thoughts have brought about certain situations in your life, your awareness shifts to a level where blind attachment to the physical workings of the world is no longer your dominant thought process. You begin to see and know that everything around you is the temporary creation of thought. You recognize that you have chosen to come into this dimension, and your search for answers to many spiritual questions begins.

You are not just creating in this physical realm. Everything you think, say, do, and feel is vibrating on multidimensional levels. You are constantly sending out messages through your feelings, thoughts, and subsequent experiences. Many self-help books advocate repeating affirmations to bring about a change in your beliefs and understandings, which can take great intensity of thought and energy. A more powerful approach and the central theme of some manifestation courses and books is to get into the feeling of what it is you wish to bring into your life. This is like sending an energetic order to the creative energies of consciousness and then allowing those energies to fulfill your order.

Even if you believe wholeheartedly in what you are intending to manifest, your subconscious beliefs can override your conscious intentions and affirmations. Therefore, any way that you can align your conscious and subconscious beliefs helps in what you are looking to create in your life. Deep meditation, some forms of self-hypnosis, and the practice of PSYCH-K — a subconscious belief change technique — are ways of aligning conscious and subconscious beliefs.

As you increase your ability to control your thoughts and associated creative ability here on Earth, successfully experiencing the instant thought environment of the hereafter naturally follows. Life is always what you make it. Your experiences of life on Earth and in the hereafter are limited only by your willingness to explore and your creative powers of imagination.

There is no hiding from your thoughts or your actions. They show on your face and in the energy that is around you. Some may be better at hiding these energy emanations than others. Yet, when you die and you no longer have a physical body, your energy is there without its protective shell for everyone else to see. What you see and feel when you die is solely determined by who you now are and what you are now doing.

You die when you have experienced all that this life has to offer. You die to further your development. You die to gather experience of what an energetic transition involves. Your death is the greatest learning opportunity of your life. When you are no longer able or willing to learn from life, then you will learn from death.

Separation Consciousness and Unity Consciousness

Our physical existence on Earth is currently based mainly around separation. "Separation consciousness" stresses an individual or collective identity that focuses on differences and keeps you from experiencing your expanded self. Your appearance, your clothes, your place of birth, the sports team you support, and the car you drive can all be part of maintaining a separate identity. Seeing yourself as fundamentally different from others creates a sense of detachment from people and from the world as a whole.

Separation consciousness is an attachment to aspects of the external world that you take on as your own. It is born from beliefs of inadequacy and lack. It seeks fulfillment through external attachments and gratification. Yet these do not satisfy the desires for wholeness. The opposite of separation consciousness is "unity consciousness." It seeks a sense of oneness first with oneself, then with others, and ultimately with all of existence.

Strong beliefs held by a large number of people create an environment, a consensus reality, and a way of being here on Earth that can be difficult for an individual to break free from. Yet, in your journey of spiritual growth and advancement, that is exactly what you are doing. You are moving on from beliefs that no longer resonate with you and finding another group of people, or tribe, that is more aligned with where you now are. In time, you will also most likely move on from this group to another one that is new and different.

Oneness with oneself is a process of dissolving the boundaries between you and the world around you, leading to a profound sense of connection, wholeness, peace, and joy. It is attained through practices such as mindfulness and other forms of self-awareness. Through these, you observe your thoughts and feelings without judgment, reducing over time the sense of separation between you and your experiences. It involves letting go of the rigid identification with the ego or personal identity, leading to a growing awareness of a greater sense of self. It is an embracing of wholeness that includes recognition and acceptance of all aspects of you, seeing yourself as a unified whole. Through ongoing meditation, contemplation, and spiritual practices, you come to experience a more profound sense of connection with others and with all of existence, experiencing yourself as part of something greater.

As your consciousness expands and your awareness heightens, you begin to realize that there is no longer a separation between you and your thoughts, between you and your words, between you and your deeds. Then you realize that there is no separation between you and the world around you. Nothing happens by accident. Everything and everyone is connected, and every encounter and experience is significant. This is the state of oneness that spiritual teachers talk about, which may at times have felt like some illusory state of being. When you realize this state of oneness, even if only for a few moments, you begin to bring it into your everyday life, in your thoughts, words, and actions, and in how you are with people and the world around you.

The point of oneness resides deep within you. There is nothing that is outside of you. It is all you. You are always connected to this internal point of oneness, of stillness. When you let go of all personal identity, you are inevitably drawn to and merged with the very essence of who you are and who everyone and everything is.

This concept was beautifully expressed by the spiritual teacher Sri Krishnamurti when he said, "What you are, the world is. And without your transformation, there can be no transformation of the world" (Krishnamurti 1947). It is a reminder that everything starts and ends with you. It is a statement that the oneness of which others speak and which you seek starts with you. There are no others to blame. There is only you. This is the ultimate meaning and purpose of the expansion of consciousness, of which you are the most important part.

The life that you are now living is part of this expansion of consciousness, with both individual and collective aspects. In the Spirit World, before you were born, you learned to see new possibilities and operate with a new awareness. When you came to this physical realm of Earth, it was with the intention of seeing differently, of experiencing energy and creation in a different way. You may have forgotten your original intention for coming to Earth. You may have been distracted by the many aspects of living. Yet, as soon as you begin asking what life is about, you are opening a door to the awareness that you are seeking. Through this seeking, your reason for existing reveals itself.

When you have reached the stage where you feel that you have much of your inner work done, you will find that your thoughts turn to your fellow humans. As you become clearer and gain wisdom and understanding, a desire to assist others in whatever way you can arises in you. You will seek to do this without reward and without recognition. This call to devote your life to the selfless service of others through nurturing a giving and loving nature is one that many spiritual masters and teachers, past and present, have chosen. This is a choice from pure unconditional love. This is a choice for life. This is a choice that transcends death. It is a choice that gives life to death.

Chapter 27

The Death of Death

There is no death. There is only life. You cannot kill anything. You can only transform its energy. In the words of ancient Taoist philosopher Chuang Tzu, "Birth is not a beginning, death is not an end. There is existence without limits; there is continuity without a starting point."

Death dies for you when you have transcended all aspects of you that keep you tied to the physical and have moved into a state where you realize that death is just a transition. Getting to this stage takes learning and change. We are all on that path of discovery and evolution. Throughout this book, we have considered many aspects of death and have risen above our fears about them. To exist fully in the state of loving death, a final consideration of some of what contributes to choosing fear over love in life's greatest transition reinforces the pathway to loving death.

Fear

Moving from fear to love is not about avoiding fear but about transforming your relationship to it. Becoming aware of your fears is your first step. Fear thrives in the unconscious, so when you recognize that you are in fear, you are bringing light to the situation. Many of the fears of death stem from other fears, such as fear of loss, failure, or of leaving the known behind.

When you become aware that you are feeling fear of death, look to see if it is a fear of something else. Meet your feelings with kindness, compassion, and non-judgment. If you become aware that your fear may originate elsewhere, seek ways to work through it and alleviate it. Seek professional help if you are unsure what to do. The aim of working through any fear is to shift you into a mastery of your fears and then into the liberating state of fearlessness.

Loss

Loss is linked to fear. Fear of death can stem from a loss of life; fear of rejection from a loss of being loved or belonging; and fear of change from the loss of the well-known or safe. Feelings of loss are founded in the fear of things being taken, of endings, of not having, or of letting go.

Loss can also be related to grief, and grief is not always about fear. Sometimes it is about love. It can be aching proof that something mattered. Being aware of the basis for your feelings of loss opens you up to understanding loss. There is no benefit in seeking to get back what has been lost. It ties us to the past, whereas we must live in the present.

When you realize that what you were previously attached to has changed, you also know that your relationship with it must change. Feelings of loss are an opportunity to focus on the space that has been created and to seek to fill it in a new way. In doing this, you are not only understanding death but also moving beyond death.

Forgiveness

Forgiveness is one of the factors that can make death and the dying process fearful. Yet it is one of the most powerful actions that you can take for yourself and others. Forgiveness moves you from anger and fear to a state of love. Forgiving those who have hurt you frees you to focus on what you love rather than what may have dominated your thoughts, words, and actions in the past. Forgiveness is about letting go and becoming free. When you let go, you create the space for something new and more wonderful to come into your life.

Love and forgiveness are deeply interconnected. Holding on to resentment, bitterness, or anger over death or some action in life creates an environment of negative emotions and fear. Love involves a willingness to forgive. Forgiveness is part of loving death. In life and death, forgiveness frees you to live life fully and love death fully.

Self-Importance

To progress here on Earth and in the hereafter involves a progressive letting go of your sense of self-importance. It entails letting go of all attachments to who you think you are. This includes the thinking that describes you, and all the things that you have accumulated around you that serve to create your identity.

Feelings of self-importance are not inherently negative, as we all need a healthy sense of self-worth. But when self-importance veers into ego inflation or superiority, it can erode deeper freedom, connection, and growth. It can also be a barrier to you accessing that place of loving death. Self-importance seeks to defend itself against anything that it thinks will deplete it. It clings to identity, to image, to unfinished stories, all of which can create fear, regret, or restlessness at the edge of life.

Death is sometimes seen as the enemy of self-importance, as it appears to negate who you are. But, as you progress on your spiritual path, you will come to know and experience that "there is no me," there just is, and I am it. As you practice letting go, more of your true self is revealed. You become familiar with the authentic feeling of freedom that is not tied to any aspect of you. The death of death comes through the awareness of impermanence, of letting go and merging back into something greater than the individual self.

Inhibitions

Freedom from inhibitions is an essential part of loving death. Inhibitions are internal barriers that prevent someone from acting freely or expressing themselves fully. Thoughts of the fear of death can trigger self-protective or defensive responses. The inhibitions of death are those behavioral mechanisms that arise in response to the presence of death. These inhibitions are not about death itself but about how thoughts of death and dying trigger self-protective, avoidant, or defensive responses in individuals and societies.

Letting go of inhibitions requires a combination of self-awareness, emotional expression, and practical exercises. Expressing your authentic self without the need for approval or rejection helps release inhibitions. Moving fully into the freedom of uninhibited exploration of life and the hereafter involves approaching all unresolved inner issues, imbalances, and conflicts with a view to letting go and finding a balanced approach to life's events.

Freedom from inhibitions is not about recklessness: it's about embracing your true self without needing to apologize. When uninhibited, you are more in the present moment, and you feel alive and joyful. When uninhibited about death, you see death as something beneficial rather than something to be feared or avoided. When you release your inhibitions, you transcend the fears of death. In transcending the fears of death, you hasten the death of death.

Gratitude

Gratitude is a powerful way to move from fear to love as it shifts your focus, emotional state, and mindset. Fear is often rooted in worries about the future or regrets about the past. Gratitude, on the other hand, grounds you in the present moment by encouraging you to notice and appreciate what you have right now. This present-moment awareness quietens the "worst-case scenario" stories that fear creates, making it harder for fear to dominate your thoughts.

Gratitude and fear are energetically opposed; you cannot fully experience both at the same time. When you practice gratitude, you activate feelings of hope, trust, and openness, which are qualities associated with love. Equally, gratitude practices diminish anxiety, worry, and doubt, which are rooted in fear.

When you act from fear, your motivation is often avoidance or self-protection. Shifting to a mindset of gratitude moves your motivation towards love and appreciation, inspiring positive actions and nurturing self-care instead of fear or self-criticism. Recognizing the benefits and beauty of death is an expression of thankfulness for its role in life. Being grateful for death is life-giving. Gratitude drives a nail into the coffin of death and precipitates the death of death.

The Evolution of Death

As humanity evolves, current truths are superseded by higher truths, and each generation brings new understanding and awareness. The widely held current view that death is a terrible and often tragic happening does not give enough credence to our true nature or to the reality of what awaits us after we leave the physical body.

Just as humanity is evolving, so too is death. The evolution of death is shaped by the evolution of humanity, and the evolution of humanity is shaped by your evolution. As you are working through your inner issues, you also move to address and alter your relationships with people and your environment. When you become clearer through resolving your inner conflicts and issues, you become more attuned to the subtle energies surrounding you and the limitless possibilities for using these energies to create whatever you choose. The concept that "if you believe it, then it is true for you" puts you in the place of the creator. You are the creator of your reality, here in the physical and wherever you go beyond the physical.

In this physical reality, it is easy to be caught up in the collective thinking around what is happening. If you believe that death is our biggest problem, then informing yourself about all aspects of death will broaden your outlook on what death is all about. The deeper you go into exploring death and the hereafter, the greater your awareness becomes of all of existence. The acceptance and embracing of the reality of existence beyond this physical reality may come to you from the contents of this book, from your research, from your intuition, or from firsthand experiences around death.

On a deep level somewhere within you, there is a profound knowing that who you are is more than just some whimsical presence in a chaotic world. The answers to who you are and what death is about lie within you. Death is an aspect of your life source. When you find and connect with your life source, you are one with infinite, unconditional love. In this love, death holds no fear for you. Through this love, death has no life. For love is eternal, and you are infinite. You are the flow of eternal love, revealing itself through the infinite you. You are life. You are the death of death.

THE END (of Death)

Chapter 28

The Death Teachings

The "death teachings" are those insights and wisdom that flow from a deeper understanding of death and its place and purpose in your spiritual evolution. When put together, they offer a profound depth of wisdom and insight into life and death. The death teachings, as detailed elsewhere in this book, are as follows.

Death Is Your Guru

Death is your teacher. Learn from death. Seek the wisdom of death in every moment. Understanding death brings an understanding of life. When you make death your constant companion, you have a friend for life. When you become comfortable with death, its inherent teachings of a fulfilled life are revealed to you.

Life Is a Spiritual Education

The experiences that you have while in physical existence here on Earth are all experiences for your spiritual development. When you are born on Earth, you enter and merge with a physical body and mind. It takes practice to master the workings of a physical body in a dense physical environment. Over time, you learn to integrate and manage all the thoughts, emotions, and physical activities that having a body entails. At death, you graduate from the school of life and are ready to move on to your next spiritual experience.

You Are Part of Spiritual Evolution

The primary reason for incarnation is to have experiences, make choices, and expand consciousness through being part of creation in every thought, word, and deed. Everything you think, say, and do contributes to the greater advancement of humanity.

You Chose Your Experiences to Evolve

All the experiences that you have contribute to your learning. You chose your life experiences so that you would have an opportunity to choose how to respond to them. The choices you make are a critical aspect of your learning experiences. You always have a choice as to how to be and what to do. No matter what is happening, you can choose to change how you respond. When you choose differently from previously ingrained habits that were detrimental to ones that are beneficial, you have mastered that experience.

Every experience is a doorway to a journey of self-exploration and awareness. This journey goes right to the core of your being and opens into the heart of all of creation. When you have experienced all that you chose before birth, you are ready to return to your spiritual existence.

Life Is a Game

Most accounts of the hereafter say that it feels more real than life on Earth. That is because it is. This life is not as real as the hereafter because this life is a form of advanced virtual reality where you decide before entering what character you will play and what experiences you will have. You decided to forget that you chose this life to see how you would be at playing the game of evolving your awareness. As your awareness grows, you are accessing higher states of awareness and starting to remember who you are and that the purpose of this game of life is to choose to love more.

See Life as a Whole

Life includes everything. Life includes death. Death is a point in time in your ongoing evolution and growing awareness of who you are and your understanding of the overall nature of existence. See all of life as a whole, rather than separate parts, some of which can be avoided or denied. When you embrace all of life, including death, you are opening to experiencing all your feelings about your death, and in the process, you feel more alive.

Everything Is Connected

You are never separate from anyone or anything. There is an energy field of consciousness that enables communication in the nonphysical and physical realms. It also facilitates communication with deceased loved ones. Your journey through the nonphysical fields of communication opens up a vista of traveling to whatever realm you choose, both now and when your physical body is dead. One of the benefits of being open to accessing other realms is that you don't have to be dead to have experiences beyond the physical. You can experience death without dying, and you can love it.

Everything Is Significant

Accounts from those who have experienced the hereafter regularly mention that even the smallest thing that happens in your life is significant. Every experience that you have, every person that you meet, and everything that is currently around you is there for a reason. The reason is for you to choose how to be and how to respond. Your response can be any of a range of emotions from fascination, wonder, and love to frustration, anger, fear, and more. How you choose to see what is happening for you feeds into your state of awareness.

Change Is Always Happening

The only constant is change, yet so much of what we see around us are attempts to keep things the same, such as the aging physical body or our financial arrangements. Death is a great change. One of the main aspects of understanding and benefiting fully from the death experience is to know that everything is always changing. Nothing stays the same.

Allow Change

The secret of living with change is not to reject it or accept it but to allow it to happen. Allow things to get broken. Allow people to come into and leave your life. Allow the many small deaths that happen every day to occur. When you become accustomed to allowing change to happen, you also allow death to happen. You then begin to embrace and love the transitions that change and death create. You see the vibrancy of life in the endings and the beginnings. You see that the circle of life has no beginning and no end.

You Are Not Your Body

You are the consciousness that animates your body. When you see yourself as a separate entity from your body, you become more of an observer of what is happening with the body. You know that what happens to the body is an experience to be considered. In this consideration, you have the opportunity to choose your response. You have an opportunity to be a master of yourself and the world through the medium of the body.

Everything Is Here and Now

Life on Earth places some restrictions on our everyday perceptions. Life on Earth is experienced through a created filter of time and space. You experience creation in a linear fashion. Yet, as you progress on your spiritual journey, you begin to realize that everything exists in one place and time. Everything is here and now. You also only ever exist in this one place and time, in the here and now. There is only now. There is no past or future; just now.

Experience the Present Moment Fully

Your spiritual evolution will not happen by focusing on the past or the future. The more you live in the present moment, the more you are open to realizing your true essence. The power of knowing and understanding this is that you become fully aware of what you are creating. When you focus your attention on the here and now, you are the active creator of your reality.

Your Thoughts Create Your Reality

Where your thoughts go, your energy follows. That is true for this life and for the hereafter. What you focus on grows. You are a powerful creator. You cause everything that happens to you. You create your world and everything that happens in it. You, and only you, control your life. Life is about making wiser choices.

Remember Who You Are

Remember who you are as a spiritual being and live your life from that remembering. Remember that all aspects of you merge into the full wholeness of yourself. Remember that who you truly are is connected to everything. You are an infinite being, an infinite consciousness, part of the greater whole of creation.

Express Gratitude

Gratitude is a stepping stone to being in a permanent state of love. You cannot be in fear when you are expressing gratitude. Being grateful is the feeling of appreciation and thankfulness for all that you experience. Feeling grateful for one thing prompts you to seek other things for which you are grateful. Gratefulness spreads and readily appears wherever you look for it.

The practice of acknowledging and expressing gratitude for all that your body is doing for you shifts you into a place of love for the body. Just as you might thank an old suit of clothes for the pleasure and service they have given you through wearing them, also thank your physical body for the service it is providing for you. And when you are ready to leave the body in death, giving thanks for all that the body has enabled you to experience keeps you in a state of love.

It is relatively easy to be grateful for life. But, because of the collective fear around death, being grateful for death currently takes consideration and commitment. When you are grateful for death, you experience a greater understanding of death and a greater zest for life. When you are grateful for death, you lose your fear of death. When you are grateful for death, you love death.

Love More

The central message from most people who have had death experiences is to love more. If you are wondering how you can love everything that happens to you and that you see happening in the world, you start by changing your perspective. See everything that is happening for people, and for humanity, as experiences for growth and opportunities to choose differently.

When you change your perspective, your life changes accordingly. The events that you see and hear about in the daily news can be a trap that ensnares you in the physical existence of this world. You do not know what others have chosen to experience for themselves. They may not even remember. Everyone is doing the best they know at whatever level of awareness they are operating. Everything you observe is a prompt to choose to love more.

Loving more encompasses gratitude, embracing change, choosing love over fear, and above all, loving yourself. Each one of these is related to how you approach death, and how you approach death is how you approach life. The first and the final teaching, with life and with death, is "You Gotta Love it."

Celebrate Death

Celebrate my passing.
Rejoice in the love that I AM
and the joy that I AM.
You have lost nothing.
You have gained an experience of change
to add to every other moment of change in your life.
I am still with you.
We cannot be separated, for we are One.

Appendix

Death Wish Checklist Example

The setting

Establish an atmosphere conducive to your passing, including:

- A quiet room – not a time for talk among people there present
- Low-level lighting

Who to have present

Choose who you wish to be present as witnesses to your transition. Choose only those who you consider will support your transition:

- Your Anam Cara (Soul Friend)
- Other loved ones present; ask them in advance
- Other spiritual friends who will hold space for you

Altar

Prepare an altar on which you can place special items, for example:

- Images of the deities, ascended masters, enlightened beings, spiritual teachers
- Sacred symbols, e.g. the flower of life, Om, Sri Yantra
- A lighted candle
- The four elements: earth, air, fire, water
- Other symbolic items

Music

Choose high-vibrational music pieces that will help maintain you in a high-vibrational state, such as:

- Mantras, sacred chants, hymns, etc.
- Other sounds, e.g. singing bowls, tingsha bells

Have a recording made in advance of the music you would like.

Affirmations

Have a recording made (or have someone read) statements that will assist you in your transition. You could include the instruction: "Please read the following statements to me as I am losing consciousness, with long quiet breaks in between."

Some you may wish to have read only once, while others you may wish to have spoken or played repeatedly. Examples for statements to be read once, or repeatedly, might be:

> "I release all attachments to the physical world and to my physical body."
> "I forgive everyone who feels that they need my forgiveness."
> "I am grateful for all the life experiences that I have had in this physical life."
> "Go to the clear light of Source."
> "Love and be loved."

Guidance for those attending:

Focus on my spiritual self. Do not focus on the human physical body that you see before you. Rather, see me for the spiritual energy that is inhabiting the body and about to leave the body. Know that this is not an ending but a transition to another state of consciousness.

Be comfortable with my death. Be at ease with yourself as I leave my physical body. The more comfortable you are with the natural process of dying, the more you will experience the amazing and beautiful transition of me leaving the body. This allows you to participate more deeply in the ultimate spiritual experience that bridges physical life and the beyond.

References

Afterlife Research and Education Institute, Inc. (no date) *Self-Guided Afterlife Connections*. Available at: https://afterlifeinstitute.org/self-guided (Accessed: 17 March 2025).

Alexander, E. (2012) *Proof of Heaven*. London: Piatkus.

Anam-Áire, P. (2021) *The Last Ecstasy of Life: Celtic Mysteries of Death and Dying*. Rochester, VT: Findhorn Press.

Atwater, P.M.H. (2021) *The Big Book of Near-Death Experiences: The Ultimate Guide to the NDE and Its Aftereffects*. Virginia Beach: Rainbow Ridge Publishing.

Bache, C. (2019) *LSD and the Mind of the Universe*. Rochester, VT: Park Street Press.

Barrett, F. & Barrett, W. (2020) *Personality Survives Death: After-Death Communication from Sir William Barrett*. Guildford: White Crow Books.

Barrett, W. (1926) *Death-Bed Visions*. London: Methuen & Co.

Bashar Communications, Inc. (2025) *Bashar.org*. Available at: https://bashar.org/ (Accessed: 9 April 2025).

Blackman, S. (1997) *Graceful Exits: How Great Beings Die: Death Stories of Tibetan, Hindu & Zen Masters*. New York: Weatherhill.

Brinkley, D. (1994) *Saved by the Light*. London: Piatkus.

Buhlman, W. (1996) *Adventures Beyond the Body*. New York: HarperOne.

Buhlman, W. (2001) *The Secret of the Soul*. New York: HarperCollins.

Buhlman, W. (2013) *Adventures in the Afterlife*. Millsboro, DE: Osprey Press.

Buhlman, W. (2016) *Higher Self Now*. Millsboro, DE: Osprey Press.

Burpo, T. & Vincent, L. (2010) *Heaven Is for Real: A Little Boy's Astounding Story of His Trip to Heaven and Back*. Nashville: Thomas Nelson.

Callanan, M. & Kelley, P. (2012) *Final Gifts: Understanding the Special Awareness, Needs, and Communications of the Dying*. New York: Simon & Schuster.

Campbell, T.C. (2003) *My Big TOE: Awakening, Discovery, Inner Workings*. Huntsville, AL: Lightning Strike Books.

Charbonier, J.-J. (2012) *Seven Reasons to Believe in the Afterlife*. Rochester, VT: Inner Traditions.

Cockell, J. (1993) *Yesterday's Children: The Extraordinary Search for My Past Life Family*. London: Piatkus.

Cockell, J. (1996) *Past Lives, Future Lives*. London: Piatkus.

Dass, R. (2000) *Still Here: Embracing Aging, Changing, and Dying*. New York: Riverhead Books.

Dhrolma, D. (2002) *Delog: Journey to Realms beyond Death*. Varanasi: Pilgrims Publishing.

Dossey, L. (1989) *Recovering the Soul: A Scientific and Spiritual Approach*. New York: Random House.

Dyer, W. & Garnes, D. (2015) *Memories of Heaven*. Carlsbad: Hay House.

Eadie, B.J. (1992) *Embraced by the Light*. Placerville, CA: Gold Leaf Press.

Easwaran, E. (trans.) (2007) *The Bhagavad Gita*. 2nd edn. Tomales, CA: Nilgiri Press.

Ferguson, A. (2011) *Zen's Chinese Heritage: The Masters and Their Teachings*. Somerville, MA: Wisdom Publications.

Ford, H. (1928) Interview in *San Francisco Examiner*, 26 August.

Gallup, G. (1982) *Adventures in Immortality: A Look beyond the Threshold of Death*. New York: McGraw-Hill.

Grey, M. (1985) *Return from Death: An Exploration of the Near-Death Experience*. London: Arkana.

Grimes, R. (2010) *The Fun of Dying*. Madison: Christine F. Anderson Publishing.

Guggenheim, B. & Guggenheim, J. (1996) *Hello from Heaven! A New Field of Research — After-Death Communication — Confirms That Life and Love Are Eternal*. New York: Bantam Books.

Heagerty, N. Riley (2015) *The French Revelation: Voice to Voice Conversations with Spirits through the Mediumship of Emily S. French*. Guildford: White Crow Books.

Hogan, C. (2020) *Your Eternal Self: Science Discovers the Afterlife*. Normal, IL: Greater Reality Publications.

IrishCentral (n.d.) *Jenny Cockell: English Woman "Reincarnated" from Irish Mum*. Available at: https://www.irishcentral.com/culture/jenny-cockell-reincarnation-irish-children (Accessed: 31 March 2025).

Keane, C. (2009) *Going Home: Irish Stories from the Edge of Death*. Bray, Wicklow: Capel Island.

Keane, C. (2010) *The Distant Shore: More Irish Stories from the Edge of Death*. Bray, Wicklow: Capel Island.

Keane, C. (2017) *We'll Meet Again: Irish Deathbed Visions: Who You Meet When You Die*. Waterford: Capel Island Press.

Keen, C., Murray, C., & Payne, S. (2013) "Sensing the presence of the deceased: A narrative review." *Mental Health, Religion & Culture*, 16(4), pp. 384–402.

Krishnamurti, J. (1947) *11th Public Talk, Madras, 28 December 1947*. Available at: https://jkrishnamurti.org/content/madras-11th-public-talk-28th-december-1947/1947 (Accessed: 12 May 2025).

Kübler-Ross, E. (1969) *On Death and Dying*. New York: Macmillan.

Lee, P.W. (2020) *Choose to Believe: A Story of Miracles, Healing, and the Afterlife*. Eagle, ID: Ladybug Media.

Leininger, B. & Leininger, A. (2010) *Soul Survivor: The Reincarnation of a World War II Fighter Pilot*. New York: Grand Central Publishing.

Levine, S. (1982) *Who Dies?* New York: Anchor Books.

Longaker, C. (1997) *Facing Death and Finding Hope: A Guide to the Emotional and Spiritual Care of the Dying*. New York: Random House.

Malachi, T. (2005) *Gnosis of the Cosmic Christ*. Woodbury, MN: Llewellyn.

McKay, M. (2021) *The Luminous Landscape of the Afterlife*. Rochester, VT: Park Street Press.

Medhus, E. (2015) *My Life after Death: A Memoir from Heaven*. Hillsboro, OR: Beyond Words Publishing.

Meyer, M. (2004) *The Gospel of Thomas: The Hidden Sayings of Jesus*. San Francisco: Harper, Saying 18.

Moody, R. (2011) *Glimpses of Eternity: An Investigation into Shared Death Experiences*. London: Rider & Co.

Moody, R.A. (1975) *Life After Life*. New York: Bantam Books.

Moody, R.A. & Perry, P. (1993) *Reunions: Visionary Encounters with Departed Loved Ones*. New York: Villard Books.

Newton, M. (1994) *Journey of Souls: Case Studies of Life between Lives*. St Paul, MN: Llewellyn.

Newton, M. (2009) *Memories of the Afterlife*. St Paul, MN: Llewellyn.

Osis, K. & Haraldsson, E. (2012) *At the Hour of Death: A New Look at Evidence for Life after Death*. Guildford: White Crow Books.

Ostaseski, F. (2017) *The Five Invitations*. London: Bluebird Pan Macmillan.

Perl, S. (2022) *Sheriperl*. Available at: http://www.sheriperl.com (Accessed: 16 March 2025).

Psi Encyclopedia (n.d.) *Dorothy Eady*. Available at: https://psi-encyclopedia.spr.ac.uk/articles/dorothy-eadyomm-sety-reincarnation-case (Accessed: 31 March 2025).

Puryear, H.B. (1982) *The Edgar Cayce Primer: Discovering the Path to Self-Transformation*. New York: Bantam Books.

Randall, E.C. (1906) *Life's Progression: Research in Metapsychics*. Buffalo, NY: The Henry B. Brown Co.

Redfield, J., Murphy, M., & Timbers, S. (2016) *God and the Evolving Universe*. London: Arrow Books.

Ring, K. & Cooper, S. (1999) *Mindsight: Near-Death and Out-of-Body Experiences in the Blind*. Palo Alto, CA: William James Center for Consciousness Studies.

Rinpoche, S. (1992) *The Tibetan Book of Living and Dying*. London: Rider-Random House.

Ritchie, G. (1978) *Return from Tomorrow*. Grand Rapids: Revell Books.

Robsahm, C. (2011) *Memoirs of Swedenborg*. Translated by A. Hallengren. Edited by S. McNeilly. London: The Swedenborg Society.

Sartori, P. (2014) *The Wisdom of Near-Death Experiences: How Understanding NDEs Can Help Us Live More Fully*. Oxford: Watkins Publishing.

Schwartz, G.E. & Simon, W.L. (2002) *The Afterlife Experiments: Breakthrough Scientific Evidence of Life after Death*. New York: Atria Books.

Schwartz, R. (2007) *Your Soul's Plan*. Berkeley, CA: North Atlantic Books.

Seek Reality (n.d.) *Verified Recordings of People Living in the Afterlife*. Available at: https://seekreality.com/seek-reality-news/verified-recordings-of-people-living-in-the-afterlife/ (Accessed: 5 April 2025).

Sigwart (1972) *The Bridge over the River*. Translated by J. Wetzl. New York: Anthroposophic Press.

Sivananda, S.S. (1946) *What Becomes of the Soul after Death*. Uttarakhand: The Divine Life Society.

Stevenson, I. (1997) *Where Reincarnation and Biology Intersect*. Westport, CT: Praeger.

Stolp, M.V. (2017) *What Happens When We Die: Our Journey in the Afterlife*. Forest Row, East Sussex: Temple Lodge.

Surviving Death (2021) Directed by Ricki Stern. [Online streaming service]. Available at: Netflix (Accessed: 17 March 2025).

Taylor, S. (2021) *Extraordinary Awakenings: From Trauma to Transformation*. Novato, CA: New World Library.

The In Between with Jim Bruton (2021) [The In Between]. *Gaia*. Available at: https://www.gaia.com (Accessed: 17 March 2025).

Thurman, R. (1994) *The Tibetan Book of the Dead*. New York: HarperCollins.

Times of India (2005) "Rebirth: Girl tracks old parents," 4 October 2005. Available at: https://timesofindia.indiatimes.com/india/rebirth-girl-tracks-old-parents/articleshow/1251545.cms (Accessed: 17 March 2025).

Tolle, E. (1997) *The Power of Now: A Guide to Spiritual Enlightenment*. Novato, CA: New World Library.

Tolle, E. (2005) *A New Earth: Awakening to Your Life's Purpose*. London: Penguin Books.

Tyrrell, R.Y. & Purser, L.C. (1904–19) *The Correspondence of M. Tullius Cicero: Arranged According to Its Chronological Order, with a Revision of the Text, a Commentary, and Introductory Essays*. Dublin: Hodges, Figgis, & Co.; London: Longmans, Green, & Co.

Van Lommel, P., van Wees, R., Meyers, V., & Elfferich, I. (2001) "Near-death experience in survivors of cardiac arrest: A prospective study in the Netherlands." *The Lancet*, 358(9298), pp. 2039–45.

Virgil (1999) *The Eclogues and Georgics*. Translated by C. Day Lewis. Oxford: Oxford University Press.

Wagner, S. (2019) "All You Need to Know about Electronic Voice Phenomena." *Liveabout.com*. Available at: https://www.liveabout.com/all-about-electronic-voice-phenomena-2594007 (Accessed: 17 March 2025).

Weiss, B. (2000) *Only Love Is Real*. New York: Grand Central Publishing.

Wright, R. & Hogan, R.C. (2011) *Guided Afterlife Connections: They Come to Change Lives*. Greater Reality Publications.

Yogananda, P. (1946) *Autobiography of a Yogi*. Los Angeles: Self-Realization Fellowship.

YouTube (2014) *Reincarnation — Gus Taylor*. 12 February. Available at: https://www.youtube.com/watch?v=vcx4rfCHqSY (Accessed: 17 March 2025).

Ziewe, J. (2008) *Multi-Dimensional Man*. Self-published. Available at: https://www.multidimensionalman.com/ (Accessed: 17 March 2025).

Ziewe, J. (2015) *Vistas of Infinity*. Self-published. Available at: https://www.multidimensionalman.com/ (Accessed: 17 March 2025).

Zohar 1:217b (Volume 1, folio 217b).

Further Reading

Dr Eben Alexander, *Proof of Heaven*

Jean-Jacques Charbonier, M.D., *Seven Reasons to Believe in the Afterlife*

Dr Brenda Davies, *Journey of the Soul*

Daniel Drasin, *A New Science of the Afterlife*

Anke Evertz, *Nine Days of Eternity*

Roberta Grimes, *The Fun of Dying*

R. Craig Hogan, *Your Eternal Self: Science Discovers the Afterlife*

Michael Newton, *Journey of Souls*

About the Author

Tony Ærcyus Christie is a Messenger of Oneness, mystic, and spiritual teacher. He brings messages and teachings of oneness through his healing and teaching work.

He left his senior management job in the Irish public service to follow his heart in the area of energy healing and sharing new information and energies that he is accessing on higher dimensions. He is founder of a new healing modality based on the labyrinth called Melchizedek Labyrinth Healing. He accesses high-vibrational energetic devices known as Golden Sphere Energetics to share with humanity.

Tony is the author of the books *Labyrinth: Your Path to Self Discovery* and *The Book of Nothing and Everything*, and the creator of the *Labyrinth Wisdom Cards*.

Tony presents workshops all over the world. He speaks at events and conferences with a view to inspiring and uplifting those present. Tony is a lifetime member of the Labyrinth Society, a qualified reflexologist, a Reiki Master, Advanced PSYCH-K facilitator, Certified Space Clearing practitioner, and a practitioner of Kriya Yoga.

Previous Titles by Tony Ærcyus Christie

Labyrinth: Your Path to Self Discovery

Labyrinth: Your Path to Self Discovery is a book that explores the labyrinth as a symbol of your path in life, providing knowledge and practical exercises to assist you on your life's journey. Discover how to work with labyrinths to quiet your mind and cultivate a sense of balance. Gain insight and answers for the issues that matter most to you. Use the labyrinth as a safe container for letting go of the worries and troubles that weigh down the mind. With the right guidance and intention, every step you take in a labyrinth can bring you greater understanding of your life's purpose and your place in the world.

Learn about the fascinating connections between the labyrinth and the Tarot, alchemy, crop circles, and the cosmos, and how they inform your path of self-discovery.

The Book of Nothing and Everything

In a world drowning in noise, this book offers silence. In an age of endless information, it presents a pause. *The Book of Nothing and Everything* is not just something to read, it's an experience to feel.

The Book of Nothing and Everything is a paradox wrapped in words. This book invites you to explore the space between words, the gap between thoughts, and the beauty of simply being. It is both a journey into nothingness and a reflection of everything, a refreshing escape from the chaos of modern life. This book is for those seeking a break from constant stimulation, deep thinkers who embrace absurdity and wonder, and anyone looking for a book that feels like an experience.

Labyrinth Wisdom Cards

Labyrinth Wisdom Cards is a deck of 48 guidance and inspirational cards inspired by the symbolism in the labyrinth, reflecting aspects of your life journey. This deck highlights the meanings embedded in the labyrinth and helps you access your inner wisdom.

These labyrinth wisdom cards will guide you to finding answers to questions, advice in difficult situations, and encouragement on your path in life. The accompanying handbook contains information about labyrinths, tells you how to use these cards, and provides additional information on the particular aspects of each wisdom card.

Note to the Reader

Thank you for purchasing *Death — You Gotta Love It*. My sincere wish is that you derive as much from reading this book as I did in creating it. If you have a few moments, please feel free to add your review of the book to your favorite online site. Also, if you would like to connect with my other books that are coming out in the near future, please visit my website for news on upcoming works, for recent blog posts, and to sign up for my newsletter: www.tonymchristie.com.

Love, Power, and Wisdom,
TONY ÆRCYUS CHRISTIE

O-BOOKS

SPIRITUALITY

O is a symbol of the world, of oneness and unity; this eye represents knowledge and insight. We publish titles on general spirituality and living a spiritual life. We aim to inform and help you on your own journey in this life. If you have enjoyed this book, why not tell other readers by posting a review on your preferred book site?

Recent Bestsellers from O-Books Are:

Heart of Tantric Sex
Diana Richardson
Revealing Eastern secrets of deep love and intimacy to Western couples.
Paperback: 978-1-90381-637-0 ebook: 978-1-84694-637-0

Crystal Prescriptions
The A-Z guide to over 1,200 symptoms and their healing crystals
Judy Hall
The first in the popular series of eight books, this handy little guide is packed as tight as a pill bottle with crystal remedies for ailments.
Paperback: 978-1-90504-740-6 ebook: 978-1-84694-629-5

Shine On

David Ditchfield and J S Jones

What if the after effects of a near-death experience were undeniable? What if a person could suddenly produce high-quality paintings of the afterlife, or if they acquired the ability to compose classical symphonies? Meet: David Ditchfield.

Paperback: 978-1-78904-365-5 ebook: 978-1-78904-366-2

The Way of Reiki

The Inner Teachings of Mikao Usui

Frans Stiene

The roadmap for deepening your understanding of the system of Reiki and rediscovering your True Self.

Paperback: 978-1-78535-665-0 ebook: 978-1-78535-744-2

You Are Not Your Thoughts

Frances Trussell

The journey to a mindful way of being, for those who want to truly know the power of mindfulness.

Paperback: 978-1-78535-816-6 ebook: 978-1-78535-817-3

The Mysteries of the Twelfth Astrological House

Fallen Angels

Carmen Turner-Schott, MSW, LISW

Everyone wants to know more about the most misunderstood house in astrology — the twelfth astrological house.

Paperback: 978-1-78099-343-0 ebook: 978-1-78099-344-7

Feng Shui Your Way to Abundance

Janine Lowe

Feng Shui Your Way to Abundance shows how to use Feng Shui to attract positive energy and change into your life.

Paperback: 978-1-80341-674-8 ebook: 978-1-80341-683-0

Naked in the Now

Marijke McCandless

What if getting present was less like work and more like being seduced by a lover?

Paperback: 978-1-80341-567-3 ebook: 978-1-80341-574-1

Crystal Creed

Jamie Inglett

A beginner's guide to learning the sacred healing powers of crystals.

Paperback: 978-1-80341-438-6 ebook: 978-1-80341-439-3

Revealing Light

Maryann Weston

YouTube psychic-astrologer Maryann Weston, from Revealing Light, shares her spiritual evolution after cancer had activated dormant psychic gifts, revealing a new purpose...

Paperback: 978-1-80341-730-1 ebook: 978-1-80341-738-7

Temple of Love

Natalie Glebova

The secret to true love is closer than you think.

Paperback: 978-1-80341-784-4 ebook: 978-1-80341-810-0

Breath for Health

A Mindful Way to Restore Your Natural Breathing Cycle

Michael D Hutchinson

Discover the secrets hidden in yoga and modern physiology — and restore your natural, healthy, confident way of breathing in just 10 minutes a day.

Paperback: 978-1-80341-440-9 ebook: 978-1-80341-441-6

Readers of ebooks can buy or view any of these bestsellers by clicking on the live link in the title. Most titles are published in paperback and as an ebook. Paperbacks are available in traditional bookshops. Both print and ebook formats are available online.

Find more titles and sign up to our readers' newsletter at **www.o-books.com**

Follow O-Books on Facebook at **O-Books**